MW00681113

A WORKBOOK IN C

A WORKBOOK IN

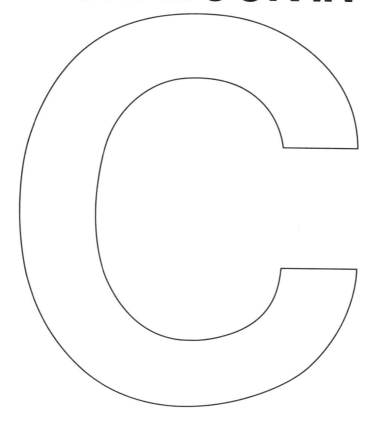

Joseph Sant

School of Computer Studies
Sheridan College

Prentice-Hall Canada Inc.
Scarborough, Ontario

Canadian Cataloguing in Publication Data

Sant, Joseph A., 1953–
  A workbook in C

Includes index.
ISBN 0-13-965468-2

1. C (Computer program language). 2. C (Computer
program language) – Problems, exercises, etc.
I. Title.

QA76.73.C15S36 1989   005.13'3   C89–093526–2

© 1989 Prentice-Hall Canada Inc., Scarborough, Ontario
All rights reserved. No part of this book may be reproduced
in any form without permission in writing from the
publisher.

Prentice-Hall, Inc., Englewood Cliffs, New Jersey
Prentice-Hall International, Inc., London
Prentice-Hall of Australia, Pty., Ltd., Sydney
Prentice-Hall of India Pvt., Ltd., New Delhi
Prentice-Hall of Japan, Inc., Tokyo
Prentice-Hall of Southeast Asia (Pte.) Ltd., Singapore
Editora Prentice-Hall do Brasil Ltda., Rio de Janeiro
Prentice-Hall Hispanoamericana, S.A., Mexico

ISBN 0-13-965468-2

Production Editor: Wendy Thomas
Production Coordinator: Sandra Paige
Design and Text Formatting: Robin Brass Studio
Cover: Robin Brass Studio

1 2 3 4 5 AP 93 92 91 90 89

Printed and bound in Canada by Alger Press

CONTENTS

INTRODUCTION

The motivation to write this workbook came from my experience in both learning and teaching C. After getting a contract to write a Computer-Aided Instruction Package that required a built-in database, I was informed that it had to be written in C. Since the project had to be developed quickly, I would have to learn C quickly. After picking up several books on C, I discovered that it was relatively hard to extract the necessary information from the books. Often, as much time was spent explaining rarely used features of the language as was spent on critical features. The explanations of binary trees and recursion were interesting but they weren't going to help me finish my project.

What I really needed, but couldn't find, was a short introduction to C that clearly explained the important features and only briefly explained the less commonly used features. This would allow me to gain a working proficiency quickly. I suspected that like other languages, the majority of the work is done using a small part of the language.

This book is designed as that quick road to a working proficiency in C. More time is spent on topics I believe are important. Less important features of C are briefly discussed for the sake of completeness. There are no b-tree's, inverted lists, or solutions to the Tower of Hanoi. Although the theory of good program design is very important, it is largely out of the scope of this book. As a result the only program design theory that will be discussed will be that which relates to the program examples.

The approach used is iterative. Initially, you will learn just enough to write a simple working program, then you will extend that knowledge to the point where you will be able to write relatively sophisticated programs. This book has many short examples to illustrate how to use the various features of C. In larger programs, it is also important to know when to use particular features. To illustrate this, there are examples at the end of several chapters—called "Putting It Together"—which explain the appropriate use of several C features within larger programs. A major case study is also provided in the last chapter.

Since the best way to learn C is by doing, exercises are provided after every chapter. Most of the program exercises take from ten minutes to one hour to complete. This book in its earlier forms was used to teach C at the junior college level and for introductory seminars for professional programmers.

Since deciding what is important in a language is very subjective, I will explain my reasoning (i.e., bias). Besides getting a taste of C and learning the basic syntax, understanding two features of C will be critical if you are to become a good C programmer:

- Functions and Storage Classes: These are the tools that will allow you to design and implement well-structured and maintainable programs.

- Pointers: This is the tool that will allow you to have sophisticated control over memory.

Once these are understood, another important feature of C is the effective use of structures. Structures can be used to reduce the logical complexity of larger programs.

This book assumes that the user has a basic knowledge of programming principles and has programmed in at least one other programming language. You should be familiar with such concepts as looping, arithmetic, decisions, simple data types and arrays.

Although this book deals primarily with ANSI C, reference is made to 'old C' when the differences between the standards are significant. ANSI C should be used in preference to 'old C' unless you are working with an old compiler.

No introduction is complete without a thank-you note to those who helped. First, I would like to thank the Research and Development Department of Sheridan College, who not only funded the original workbook, but also provided much help and encouragement. Others to thank include faculty, students, and administrative staff: Jon Duerdoth, Verna Frayne, Jim Greer, Harv Honsberger, Bob Lovelace, Lynette Morgan, Bruce Schwantz, Lisa Sutcliffe, Ding Tsuji, Joan Vinal-Cox and those students who provided suggestions or corrections in the earlier versions.

Special thanks are owed to James Burgess of Algonquin College, R. Nigel Horspool of the University of Victoria, and Barry Street of Humber College, all of whom reviewed the manuscript at different stages and offered many helpful suggestions. I would also like to thank Ed O'Connor from Prentice-Hall Canada, who carefully guided the manuscript through the various production phases.

1

A WORKING SUBSET

With most computer languages, it is necessary to know only a minimal subset of the language and some syntax rules to do productive work. By concentrating on this working subset, we will be able to quickly write and test programs. Our initial subset will consist of the following:

- Program Structure: statements, blocks
- Defining Data: integers, floating points, and characters
- Output: printf( )
- One Looping Structure: the 'while' loop
- Arithmetic Operators: +, -, /, *, ++, --
- Decisions: the 'if', the 'else';
              relational operators: ==, <, >, >=, <=, !=
- Input: scanf( )

PROGRAM STRUCTURE

All C programs consist of functions, blocks and statements. Every C program must have one `main()` function which is where the program begins executing. Look below at a working program that consists of one `main()` function which contains both statements and blocks.

```
main()
{    int   count;

     count = 1;                    ← Statement

     while ( count <= 10 )
     { printf("loop 10 times\n");      Block
       count = count + 1;              belonging
     }                                 to while
}
```

Function

1

Components of a Program

A STATEMENT is a valid C instruction followed by a ';'.

```
count  =   1;
```

A BLOCK is a method of grouping statements together. We need blocks to denote the beginning and end of code belonging to functions, 'if's, and loops. In the code below we want two statements to belong to our `while` so we must block them off using curly brackets ({ }). These curly brackets are commonly referred to as braces. Blocks may contain other blocks.

```
while ( count <= 10 )
{ printf("loop 10 times\n");
  count = count + 1;
}
```

A FUNCTION is similar to procedures and subroutines in other languages. Functions allow you to give a name to a block of code. Every program must have a `main()` function.

DATA TYPES/DECLARATIONS

Initially we will concern ourselves with only three types of data, the integer, the floating point number, and character type data. You must always declare any variable by stating its name and type before you can use it. Some of the keywords you can use to declare variable types are below.

```
float  – a floating point number
int    – a signed integer
char   – single character
```

You define a variable by listing its type first, then its data name second. Data names must begin with a letter or an underscore, and be followed by any combination of letters, underscores, or digits. Both upper- and lower-case letters are allowed but it is an unwritten rule to use only lower-case letters for variable names. In some implementations, only the first eight characters are significant.

```
float interest, principal_amt, no_of_loops;
```

You can also initialize variables when you define them by assigning them values.

```
int  limit = 40;
```

Program Using Both Integers and Floating Points
NOTE: The '%f' in our final print statement is a special format symbol which will be automatically replaced by the value of 'principal'.

```
main()
{ int   iterations;
  float principal,interest;

  iterations = 1;
  principal = 10000;
  interest  = .08;
  while ( iterations <= 10 )
    { principal = principal + (principal * interest);
      iterations = iterations + 1;
    }
  printf("principal after 10 years is %f\n", principal);
}
```

OUTPUT: THE 'printf()' FUNCTION

This is a function in the standard library used for output to the standard output device (normally the screen). It is not a true part of the C language since it is a function. It enables you to print both strings and numeric variables, but to print numeric variables you must put special characters in the string to signify that you wish them to be replaced by a number.

Printing a String Constant

```
printf("this string is in quotes\n");
```

The '\n' is the symbol for a single character called the linefeed. The next printed character will therefore start on a new line.

'\t' would cause a tab.

Printing Either Integers or Floating Points

To print variables, you must place special conversion characters within your string, and place the variables you wish printed after the string.

The conversion symbols are:

```
%c          for a character
%d          for an integer in decimal format
%f          for a floating point number
%s          for a string
```

```
int shares = 1000;
float price = 15.50;

printf("You have %d shares at %f a share\n", shares, price);
```

Output:
```
You have 1000 shares at 15.500000 a share
```

A LOOPING STRUCTURE ('while')

The while is a top checking loop that will continue performing the enclosed block until the condition specified is false. Shown below is a while loop that executes 20 times.

```
int   num = 1;
while ( num <= 20 )
{ printf("this is printed 20 times\n");
  num = num + 1;
}
```

An interesting feature of C is that relational expressions are not absolutely necessary for any loop or if. It takes any zero value to be false and any non-zero value to be true. For loops, this means that 0 means STOP, and any non-zero value means GO. The code below exhibits an infinite loop. Because only one statement is being executed no braces are needed.

```
while(1)
    printf("will this ever end\n");
```

The following program demonstrates the use of the while to determine how many years it would take for $10,000 to become $1 million when invested at a given interest rate.

```
main()
{
    int    iterations, magicyear;
    float  principal, interest;

    iterations = 0;
    principal  = 10000.0;
    interest   = .08;

    while( principal < 1000000.00 )
    {
        principal = principal + (interest * principal);
        iterations = iterations + 1;
    }
    magicyear = iterations;
    printf("your magic year is %d\n", magicyear);
}
```

ARITHMETIC / ASSIGNMENT

The simple arithmetic operators in C are similar to those in other languages (i.e., +, -, /, *).

In addition to these there is a modulus (or remainder) operator '%', which gives the remainder when one number is divided by another. Two examples are given below.

```
c = 22 % 7;
d =  7 % 22;
```

c is assigned the value 1, and d is assigned the value 7.

Increment and Decrement Operators (++ and --)

These are special operators that increment or decrement a variable by 1. You can place these operators before or after any numeric variable (i.e., ++count, or count++). Placing the operator before or after the variable can affect the result, if the variable is used in an arithmetic statement or comparison.

If the '++' is placed before the variable name, the variable will be incremented before its value is used in the arithmetic statement.

If the '++' is placed after the variable name, the original value would be used in the arithmetic statement, then after its value is used, it will be incremented.

The decrement operator works in a similar manner. Some examples are shown below.

```
int a = 4, b = 9, c, d, e;

c = ++a;
d = b++;
e = ++b;
```

In this case, 'c' is assigned the value 5, because the value of 'a' is incremented before being used; 'd' is assigned the value 9, because the value of 'b' is used before it is incremented. 'e' is assigned the value 11. Why?

```
main()
{ int    iterations = 0;
  int    limit = 5;
  int    loops = 0;

  while ( ++iterations <= limit )
            loops++;

  printf("the number of loops is %d\n", loops);
}
```

In the code above, the '++' is placed before the variable name 'iterations'. This means that 'iterations' is always incremented before it is compared against the value of 'limit' (i.e., 5). In the very first loop, iterations will be incremented from 0 to 1, then compared to 'limit'. The sequence of valid values for 'iterations' which is compared against 'limit' is 1,2,3,4,5. The total number of loops is five.

The increment operator has also been used with 'loops' to keep track of the number of loops. In this particular case, this is the equivalent of " loops = loops + 1; ". We could have used '++loops' instead of 'loops++' since we want to increment 'loops' only by one, and the value of 'loops' was not used elsewhere in the statement.

Now, what would happen if we were to place the '++' after 'iterations' (i.e., 'iterations++')? In the very first loop, the original value of 'iterations' (which is 0) is compared to 'limit', then after the comparison, 'iterations' is incremented from 0 to 1. The sequence of valid values for 'iterations' which is compared against 'limit' is 0,1,2,3,4,5. This time the number of loops is six. Because we increment after we compare, we have an extra loop.

Variables being altered through the use of these operators should not be used more than once in an expression. These operators cause the value of the variable to change during the course of the expression. This is known as a side-effect. Unfortunately, the standard for C does not specify when these values should be changed, after the entire expression has been evaluated, or immediately after the use of the operator. As a result, a statement such as 'c = a++ - ++a' will have unpredictable results.

THE 'if' STATEMENT

The `if` acts like the `if` in other languages, that is, the statement or block associated with the `if` is or is not executed depending on the truth of the condition. The condition must immediately follow the `if` and be enclosed in parentheses. Like the `while`, a relational condition is not absolutely necessary since any zero value is considered false, and any non-zero value is considered true. The relational and conjunctive operators that may be used are as follows.

Operators	Meaning
Relational	
==	equals
<	less than
>	greater than
<=	less than or equal
>=	greater than or equal
!=	not equal
Conjunctive	
&&	logical and
||	logical or
!	logical negation

The code below illustrates the use of `if` structures with simple and compound conditions, a single statement, and a block. Try not to make your compound conditions too complex, since they become very hard to understand.

Single Condition, Single Statement

```
if ( number_of_days == 31 )
   monthno++;
```

Compound Condition, Block

```
if ( number_of_days == 31  &&  month_length == 31 )
{
  month_no++;
  number_of_days = 0;
}
```

Sometimes it is easier to understand and work with the opposite of a condition rather than the condition itself. The not operator, '!', reverses the truth value of any simple or compound condition (non-zero becomes 0, and 0 becomes 1). If you are going to 'not' a compound condition, you must enclose the condition inside round brackets (parentheses). This is necessary because of the precedence of operators which is discussed in the next chapter.

As an example let's take a car sale. We want to reduce the price of all cars on our lot, except for any car with eight cylinders or any car that is a model number 3. The code using the not operator is shown below.

```
if( !( model == 3 ||  cylinders == 8))
   price = price * 0.90;
```

Notice the bracketing necessary to 'not' the entire compound condition.

Also notice that we could have performed the same task without using a '!' by using two '!=' operators.

```
if ( model != 3 && cylinders != 8 )
    price = price * 0.90;
```

A common error for new C programmers is to use '=' instead of '==' in the condition following an `if`. The compiler will assume you wish an assignment and simply test if the result of the assignment is 0 (false) or not zero (true).

As an example we will accept an integer, representing a dice roll, and test to see if it is 2, which causes the dice thrower to automatically lose his/her money. The `scanf()` in the code below is used to accept data from the keyboard (see section 1.7).

```
/*  This code doesn't work properly  */

int dice_roll = 0;

scanf("%d", &dice_roll);
if ( dice_roll = 2 )
    printf("you rolled a 2, you lose\n");
```

The code above is totally legal but, no matter what number is entered, the message is always printed out. The reason for this is that we used an assignment operator ('=') instead of a comparison operator ('=='). The compiler will assume you wish an assignment and perform an assignment instead of a comparison. Because the whole expression inside the brackets eventually evaluates to a non-zero value (2), it will be considered true.

THE 'if...else'

The `else` allows you to prescribe an action or actions if the preceding `if` condition was false. Every `else` is always paired with its closest preceding unpaired `if`. You must always be careful in setting up your `if`/`else`s because your blocking will also affect which statements will be executed.

Simple 'if...else'
```
if ( principal >= 10000 )
    interest_rate = .1075;
else
    interest_rate = .1025;
```

Nested 'if...else'
The following code compares a stock transaction to a minimum amount (2000.00). If it is below that minimum amount, a minimum charge (30.00) is assigned; otherwise, a commission rate is determined based on the price of the stock, and a charge is calculated based on the minimum charge, commission rate and number of shares.

```
int no_shares;
float transaction, stock_price, charge, com_rate;

if ( transaction < 2000.00 )
   charge = 30.00;
else
{ if ( stock_price > 20 )
      com_rate = .05;
   else if ( stock_price > 10 )
      com_rate = .04;
   else
      com_rate = .03;
   charge = 30.00 + no_shares * com_rate;
}
```

INPUT: 'scanf()'

The `scanf()` function allows us to get information from the user at the keyboard and easily convert it to any of the allowed data types. Like the `printf()` function we must use a set of conversion characters (e.g., %c, %d). Conversion codes must be provided inside the format string (inside the double quotes). The address of the variable into which you wish the input value to be deposited must be provided after the format string. We can specify the address of any variable by putting a '&' before the name of the variable we wish to use.

If we want to accept input into an integer 'idno', we would provide the conversion string "%d", and the address of 'idno', which is '&idno'. The necessary statements are shown below.

```
int idno;
scanf("%d", &idno);
```

Some of the allowable conversion codes are:

%d	signed decimal number	('int' type variable)
%f	floating point number	('float' type variable)
%c	character	('char' type variable)
%s	string	(character array)

The `scanf()` function usually separates the entered data by white space (blanks, tabs, carriage returns, etc.). If we used the `scanf()` to accept three floats from the line below (e.g., `scanf("%f%f%f", &a, &b, &c)`) it will ignore any white space between data. Please note that although we can place several inputs on one line no real conversions are done until a return or enter key is hit.

```
23.78          345.1 78.9 <enter>
```

There are some special considerations when using `scanf()` to accept characters or strings. Whenever you use the conversion code '%c' the next character from the keyboard is stored into your variable, regardless of whether it is white space or not. Look at the following statements and the results when the user inputs data.

```
char a, b, c, d;
scanf("%c%c%c%c", &a, &b, &c, &d);
```

User Enters
```
1<enter>2<enter>
```

Resulting Values
```
a    is    1
b    is    '\n'  (line feed)
c    is    2
d    is    '\n'  (line feed)
```

To accept a string you must set up an array of characters. You can do this by specifying your array name with the number of characters you need in square brackets. For strings, always specify one more character than the largest string you expect to use. This is to allow space for a string terminator. An example of reserving an array large enough to hold a ten-character name is found below.

```
char   name[11];
```

When you use `scanf()` with strings you needn't use the 'address of' operator '&' because all array names are interpreted as addresses. An example of a `scanf()` accepting a string is found below.

```
scanf("%s", name);
```

Be careful when you use '%s' with `scanf()`. First, it doesn't protect against overriding the bounds of the array. If you use `scanf()` to accept a ten-character name and the user enters 20 characters, the first ten characters will go into 'name' and the rest will wipe out the data below it.

Second, the user's input is separated (delimited) by white space, which includes blanks. You often want to have blanks included in your strings. To overcome this problem we can use the `gets()` function. It takes a full line of input (terminated by a carriage return) and deposits it into the specified character array. Once again, because it is a string you must reserve one more character than the longest string you expect to be entered. You can get only one string at a time with `gets()`:

```
char   sentence[81];
gets(sentence);
```

PUTTING IT TOGETHER

A COMMODITIES PROGRAM

We can now try to use some of the instructions we learned in this chapter to write a small program that calculates the value of two commodities, gold and silver. The value of our commodities can be calculated by multiplying the commodity price (i.e., silver_rate and gold_rate) by the amount in ounces (i.e., amount). The user will enter the commodity type and the amount.

There are a few things that should be noted in the code.

Choosing and Declaring Data Types.

'type' was declared as an integer because it represents the commodity type and should have only whole number values. All the other data items were declared `float` because they are likely to have fractional values. The declaration of the data occurred at the top of the `main()` function before they were used in any instructions.

Using 'printf()'

Our `printf()` statements included imbedded control characters such as newlines (`'\n'`) and tabs (`'\t'`), as well as substitution symbols (`'%f'`) to display the values of variables.

Using 'scanf()'

We had to use two different conversion characters (`'%d'` and `'%f'`) with `scanf()` because we were accepting an integer, then a float.

We provided the address of our variables in `scanf()` using the `'&'` operator, NOT the variable names themselves.

Using Nested 'if's'

We used a nested `if` so that we could test for an error in commodity type in addition before printing out the total value for our commodity. Most of the `if`s and `else`s controlled a single statement. One of the `else`s controlled a block (i.e., a block of code enclosed in braces). This block contained another `if` structure.

Commenting Your Program

We can include comments in a program by enclosing our explanatory text between a '/*' and a '*/'.

```
/* COMMOD.C   This program asks the user for a commodity
              type (gold or silver) and amount (ounces)
              and prints out the total value.
*/

main()
{
    int type;
    float amount;
    float total_value;
    float gold_rate = 450.00;
    float silver_rate = 7.00;

    printf("\n\t1  Gold");
    printf("\n\t2  Silver\n");
    printf("\nEnter Type of Commodity: ");
    scanf("%d", &type);
    printf("\nEnter number of ounces: ");
    scanf("%f", &amount);

    if ( type != 1 && type != 2 )
       printf("Invalid commodity type\n");
    else
       {
         if ( type == 1 )
            total_value = gold_rate * amount;
         else if ( type == 2 )
            total_value = silver_rate * amount;
         printf("The total value for your metal is %f\n",
                total_value);
       }
```

LABORATORY 1

1. Write a program to calculate the area of a circle when the user enters the radius. Prompt the user for the radius. For a refinement, put the whole process in a loop that quits when the user enters -99. The formula for the area of a circle is:

   area = 3.14159 * radius * radius

2. Write the C code for a program to convert a Fahrenheit temperature to Celsius. The user must enter the Fahrenheit temperature. Prompt the user for the temperature. For a refinement, put the whole process in a loop that quits when the user enters -99. The formula for the conversion is :

   celsius = (fahrenheit - 32) * 5.0 / 9.0

   Experiment by using the numbers 5 and 9 instead of 5.0 and 9.0.

3. Write a program that will process insurance payouts on accident claims. Have the user input the total claim and the type of claim (1, 2, 3).

   If claim type is 1, deductible is 100.00
   If claim type is 2, deductible is 200.00
   If claim type is 3, deductible is 500.00

   The formula for payout is:

   payout = total claim - deductible.

   For a refinement, validate that the claim type is correct.

4. A national park can support only 1000 deer without damage being done to the ecosystem. If the present deer population is 300 and the growth rate is 28% per year, how many years will it take before the ecosystem is damaged?

   For a refinement, consider that the wolf population is ten and its growth rate is 10%. Each wolf kills five deer per year. How many years will it take before damage is done to the forest? (For every iteration subtract wolf kills from the deer population.)

2
EXTENDING OUR SUBSET

You should now have a taste of writing simple C programs. Now we will look at extending our subset to allow more flexibility in solving problems. C is a small language, but it does provide many useful tools—the rich set of operators, the variety of data types we can use, and the small but effective set of C instructions.

MORE ON DATA TYPES AND CONSTANTS

The data types we started with were signed integers, floating point numbers, and characters. C provides several other numeric data types that you may use in your programs.

Why do we need any more numeric data types since we already have a type that stores whole numbers and one that stores fractional values? The answer is simply that more data types means more flexibility in designing efficient solutions to any problem. The questions below might help you decide on a data type.

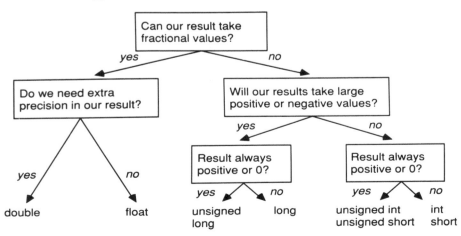

There are a few other points to note when choosing a data type.

Using a `double` instead of a `float` or a `long` instead of `int` usually requires more memory. You can always use the `sizeof` operator to determine the size of any data type. An example is shown below.

```
printf("a double takes up %d bytes\n", sizeof(double));
```

The range of a data type (i.e., the span between the lowest and highest value a type may represent) will vary from machine to machine. Sometimes the range of a variable might even vary on the same machine depending on the options you use when compiling. A brief table of data types and their typical ranges is shown below.

Data Type	Typical Small Computer	Typical Large Computer
short	-128...127	-32768...32767
int	-32768...32767	-2147483648...2147483647
unsigned int	0...65535	0...4294967295
long	-2147483648...2147483647	-2147483648...2147483647

The difference between a signed and unsigned data type is the starting point of the range. Shown below are the ranges of a short and unsigned short on most machines. In both cases the highest value is 65,535 greater than the lowest but with signed short integers we start at -32,768 and with unsigned short integers we start at 0.

	Range
short	-32,768 to 32,767
unsigned short	0 to 65,535

When you assign literals to a long integer you must place an 'L' or 'l' after the literal.

```
long  big_n;
big_n = 10500L;
```

Using Constants

Constants or literals are data items that are interpreted as they are written (e.g., 123, 78.546, "string literal"). C provides several means of writing constants for integers, floating point numbers, strings or characters.

The integer constants are the most interesting since you can denote constants in decimal form (most commonly used) or octal or hexadecimal. To use a decimal constant just write the desired number, making sure that there is no leading zero in the number, 123 (decimal 123). To use an octal constant (numbers where the base is 8 instead of 10) just provide a leading zero on your number: 0123 (octal 123 or decimal 83). Notice that 123 and 0123 denote very different values. To use hexadecimal constants add 0x before your number: 0x123 (hex 123 or decimal 291).

Real or floating point constants are provided by using a number with a decimal point in it (4.50) or by using a number in scientific notation (e.g., 1.73e4 , 1.73 times 10 raised to the power of 4).

String constants are enclosed in double quotes, "a string". One advantage of C is that you can embed any carriage control character or special character inside a string by using the backslash and either the symbol for the carriage control character or the ASCII number of the character. The following string imbeds the escape character, ASCII 27, into the string in octal form (the octal equivalent of 27 is 33).

```
"\033[2J"
```

On some systems, displaying this string will clear the screen.

There are also character constants in C. These are enclosed in single quotes, not the double quotes that are used with strings (e.g., 'a'). One must realize that a character in C is really just a very short integer. Any character constant in C, such as 'a', really represents the ASCII value of that character (e.g., 'a' is 97). In other words, when you assign 'a' to a character variable you are really assigning it the value 97.

Casting Data Types

C allows you to convert the contents of a variable of one type to another type by casting it. We might need to convert an integer into a float, or a char into an integer, for an arithmetic or a print statement. We simply put the name of the data type we wish the value to change to in parentheses (immediately before the variable name or constant). As an example, let's try to divide two integers and assign the value to a double.

```
int x = 7, y = 10;
double result;

result = x/y;
```

'result' becomes 0.0 not .70 because since both 'x' and 'y' are integers, an integer division is performed and the remainder is lost. A simple solution to this problem is to force a floating point division by casting one of the integers to a double.

```
result = (double) x/y;
```

Here, although 'x' is really an integer, for the purposes of that one statement, it will be converted into a floating point number. This automatically forces a floating point division. Note that the casting is done on 'x' before the division is performed because casting is more "important" than division (this will be discussed later in this chapter under precedence).

MORE ON OPERATORS

The Assignment Operators

We often come across statements of the form

```
principal = principal + interest;
```

C provides a short form for this type of statement using the assignment operators. Below are some examples of assignment operators and their equivalent expressions.

Operator	Example	Equivalent Expression
+=	total += 7;	total = total + 7;
-=	a -= 4 ;	a = a - 4 ;
/=	c /= (b + c);	c = c/(b + c);
*=	pop *= 1.1;	pop = pop * 1.1;
%=	t %= 3;	t = t % 3;

Conditional Assignment

We often see the case in which, if a particular condition is true, we assign a variable one value, and if it is false we assign it another value. Up to this point, we would have handled the problem using an `if...else` as shown below.

```
int  max, x = 7, y = 3;
if ( x > y )
    max = x;
else
    max = y;
```

We could have written the equivalent of this code using the conditional assignment operators. We must specify the condition to be tested followed by a '?', then state the two possible results separated by a ':'. Look at the example below. 'max' is assigned 'x' if the condition 'x > y' is true and 'y' is assigned if the condition is false. The code is an exact equivalent of the `if...else` above.

```
int  max, x = 7, y = 3;
max = x > y ? x : y ;
```

Precedence and Associativity

One of C's strengths is the great number of operators that are available. If we place several operators in the same statement, we must know how they will react within the statement. Precedence tells us how important the operator is (i.e., which operations are done first). Associativity tells us whether to start from the left or the right if two or more operators have the same precedence level. Knowing both of these will ensure that the computer performs the operations in the order that was intended. A list of operators and their precedences and associativities is found in Appendix B.

To demonstrate how different operators interact, we will try to write a code that will print out Fahrenheit conversions for Celsius temperatures between 5.0 and 100.0 in increments of 5. Our first attempt, shown below, doesn't work properly.

```
/* bad code */
float celsius = 0.0;
while ( celsius += 5.0 <= 100.0 )
    printf("Celsius %f Fahrenheit %f\n",
            celsius, 32.0 + 1.8 * celsius);
```

This code, although legal, works in a peculiar way. It creates an endless loop, but the Celsius temperature is incremented by 1.0 with each loop, and not the 5.0 we expected. Why?

The answer lies in the table of precedences in Appendix B. There are two operators in our condition, '+=' and '<='. '<=' has a higher precedence than '+=' so it will be done first. That means that '5.0 <= 100.0' is evaluated first and since this statement is always true it will always generate a truth value of 1. The '+=' causes the result of this evaluation (1) to be added to 'celsius'. This is why 'celsius' is always being incremented by 1. To correct the statement above we would enclose the part of the statement we want done first in parentheses.

```
while( (celsius += 5) <= 100.0 )
{ ..........
```

As mentioned before, associativities tell us what will happen when two or more operators with the same level of precedence occur in the same statement. Look at the example below, then look up the associativities of '/' and '*' .

```
float x;
x = 10.0/2.0 * 5.0;
```

The table of precedences states that '/' and '*' have the same level of precedence (i.e., they are equally important). Now it makes a significant difference if we start our processing from the right of the statement or the left. In one case we would get an answer of 1.0 and in the other an answer of 25.0. The associativity for these operators is 'left to right'. This means that for equally important operators, the operation on the left (10.0/2.0) will be done first. Our answer is 25.0.

You can also have 'right to left' associativity. The 'right to left' associativity of the assignment operator allows us to set several variables to the same value in one statement.

```
long  x, y, z;
x = y = z = 12345L;
```

The examples above are relatively simple when compared to some of the complex statements you might be tempted to write. That is why you should always have the table of precedences available when programming. Serious C programmers should purchase and program with one of the popular C handbooks. The other advice is,"When in doubt, bracket it." The parentheses have a very high precedence and will ensure that what is inside the parentheses is considered first. The last advice is to avoid complex statements unless absolutely necessary. Remember that, usually, what little you gain in efficiency from these complex statements, you lose in code readability and debugging time.

MORE ON LOOPS

The 'for' Loop

The for in C is a construct that allows you to easily code a counted loop. It is written as a 'for' with three statements enclosed in parentheses, and separated by a ';'.

```
for ( counter = 1; counter <= 20; counter++ )
    printf("this message is printed 20 times\n");
```

This for is the exact equivalent of the following statements:

```
counter = 1;
while ( counter <= 20 )
{
    printf("this message is printed 20 times\n");
    counter++;
}
```

An important difference between the for in C and those in other languages is that any statement, including the null statement, may be substituted for the three statements, although generally:

Statement 1 is used to initialize a counter.

Statement 2 is an expression that states under what conditions the loop will continue processing.

Statement 3 is generally used to increment a counter or pointer.

Please note that this `for` is just a convenient version of the `while` loop. The most critical part of the `for` is statement 2, the statement that indicates under what conditions the loop continues to execute. A value or expression that evaluates to either 0 or false will cause the loop to terminate, and any value or expression that evaluates to non-zero or true will allow it to continue. An example of a simple `for` loop is shown below.

```
for ( i = 1 ; i <= 100; ++i )
    printf("this is loop %d\n", i);
```

We are allowed to use any combination of null statement and non-null statements to set up our `for` loop. The example below uses three null statements and a `break` within the body of the loop. `break` is a special statement used to break out of loops (it will be discussed in more detail later in the chapter). In this case the `for` does no initialization, does not check for an exit condition, and performs no action on each loop.

```
int total = 0;
int number;

for (;;)
{ scanf("%d",&number);
  if ( number == 99 )
     break;
  else
     total += number;
}
```

You are also allowed to have multiple statements for both your initialization and incrementation by separating the statements by a comma ','. An example that does two initializations and two incrementations is shown below. Separating the initialization, looping condition, and incrementation statements of complex `for` loops onto separate lines will usually increase readability.

```
for( i = 0, j = 0;
     i < 10;
     i += 2, j += 5 )
    printf("i is %d and j is %d \n", i, j);
```

The 'do...while'

The `do...while` is very similar to the `while`, except that it always checks at the bottom of the loop. This will be used whenever you want the loop to execute at least once before quitting. A common use for bottom-checking loops is input and validation routines. The following loop executes repetitively until the user inputs a proper response.

```
int choice;

do
  {
    printf("\nselect a choice (1-5): ");
    scanf("%d", &choice);
  } while ( (choice < 1) || (choice >5) );
```

USING THE PREPROCESSOR

One of our goals in writing C programs should be that our programs are simple and easily read. The preprocessor is one tool that will help us achieve this goal. It actually goes through your code immediately before compilation and changes the code according to your instructions. These statements are usually placed at the top of your program file, and every preprocessor statement begins with a '#'. We will look at two of these statements.

'#define'

We could make our source program more readable by using meaningful names instead of numeric literals such as '12' or '1'. If we could use NO_OF_MONTHS instead of '12', and TRUE instead of '1' (if that is what they represent), our code would be much more understandable. To enable us to use meaningful names, we use #define:

```
#define   NO_OF_MONTHS   12
#define   TRUE 1
```

Now, once we have placed this at the top of the program, we could use 'NO_OF_MONTHS' wherever we would have used '12', and 'TRUE' wherever we would have used '1'. Do not put semicolons at the end of these statements; if you did, the semicolon would be substituted into your source code (along with the '12' or '1') and produce unwanted effects. An example of how we would use these symbolic literals is shown below.

```
if (  month_in < 1  ||  month_in > NO_OF_MONTHS )
    date_error = TRUE;
```

The #define is much more than a technique to 'beautify' code. One feature of many, if not most, programs is that they will have to be changed. #define can make these program changes less painful (especially in very large programs). One common reason for changing programs is that constants within the program change. As an example, let's look at a simple payroll program. There is typically a maximum limit for regular hours, after which overtime must be paid. We could write this limit into our program as a number, say 40.0, wherever it is needed in our program. If the regular work week was reduced to 37.5 hours, we would have to search through the entire program for any occurrence of the number 40.0 and determine whether it related to the regular pay limit or to something else. This trouble can be eliminated using the following #define at the top of our program and changing it when necessary.

```
#define REGULAR_LIMIT 40.0
```

'#include'

Now that we know how to use #define, we might set up a whole list of #define instructions to give names to several literals. Since these symbolic literals might be useful in other files, we might want to put all of the #define statements in a separate file, such as "symbols.h", and just include it into our source file when we want to use those symbolic literals. An example of how we would include a file at a specific point in our code is given below.

```
#include "symbols.h"
```

or

```
#include <symbols.h>
```

The only difference between the two statements above is how the search for the file to be included will be performed. If you enclose the filename in quotes, it will look for the include file in the current directory. Then if it can't find it, it will search other user-specified directories, and finally the standard locations to find include files. How you establish these standard locations is dependent on the system you use. If you enclose the filename in angle brackets it will search only the standard locations for the file. If, at any time, you provide a full path name for a file, it will search only that path.

It is common practice, when using #include, to use the double quotes for your own special include files, and angle brackets for system-supplied files. Later on we will learn about a commonly used system-supplied header file, "stdio.h", which is required for most input-output operations in C.

MORE ON INPUT AND OUTPUT

The 'printf()' Function

Special Formatting of Floats, Integers

We have already used the special formatting symbols '%f' and '%d' with printf() to print out the values of floating point numbers and integers. The numbers were always displayed in the same format (i.e., floating points were always displayed with six decimal places). We might want more control over the appearance of our output.

Some of the added features we can use are:

• Specify the MINIMUM FIELD SIZE of an integer or floating point number. The displayed number would be right justified in that field (padding on the left with blanks). We specify minimum field sizes by placing a number before the 'd' or 'f' (e.g., %7d, %10f). If more room is required to display the number properly, it will be allocated. An example is shown below.

```
int   x = 6;
float y = 7.3;
printf("%5d%10f\n", x, y);
```

Output:
```
    6  7.300000
```

- Specify the NUMBER OF DECIMAL PLACES to be displayed in a floating point number. Use a '.' followed by the number of decimal places (e.g., %7.2f, %.3f). The number will be rounded, not truncated, to the proper number of decimal places. An example is shown below.

```
float  x = 4.4567, y = 6.7890;
printf("%.2f%7.1f\n", x, y);
```

Output:
```
4.46     6.8
```

- Specify padding with zeroes instead of blanks. Place a '0' before your field length (e.g., %06d).

```
int x = 27;
printf("%06d\n", x);
```

Output:
```
000027
```

- Print out long integers. Place an 'l' before the 'd' in your printf string (e.g., %ld).

```
long big_n = 1000L;
printf("%7ld\n", big_n);
```

Output:
```
   1000
```

- Print out doubles or long floats. Place an 'l' before the 'f' in your 'printf' string (e.g., %lf).

```
double big_real = 1003423.12345678;
printf("%.8lf\n", big_real);
```

Output:
```
1003423.12345678
```

- Precision with strings. You can specify both a minimum field length and a precision when you print strings just as you did with floats. The precision of a string is the number of characters you want from the string (starting from the left of the string).

```
static char message[20] = "this is a long message";
printf("%10.7s\n", message);
printf("%.13s\n", message);
```

Output:
```
   this is
this is a lon
```

- Left justification. To align the printed characters to the left side of a field use a '-' before your field length or precision.

```
float real = 3.4;
printf("***%-10.7s***\n", message);
printf("***%-7.1f***\n", real);
```

Output:
```
***this is   ***
***3.4     ***
```

The 'puts()' Function

The puts() function simply puts a string variable or literal to the screen. It is more efficient than using printf() with a '%s' conversion symbol. puts() will append a newline, '\n', to the end of your string. Two examples are shown below.

```
char message[21];
puts(message);
puts("enclose string literals in double quotes");
```

The 'scanf()' Function

In the last chapter we used scanf() in a restricted manner to accept one of four types of data objects. scanf() provides conversion symbols to accept any one of the standard data types in C. It also provides several means of controlling the input.

Some of the additional conversion symbols (all are ANSI Standard) and the conversions they cause are listed below.

Symbol	Conversion and target data type
%o	integer in octal form to int
%x	integer in hexadecimal to int
%u	decimal unsigned to unsigned int
%lu	decimal unsigned to unsigned long int
%lf	floating point to double
%ld,lo,lx	integer in decimal, octal or hexadecimal form to long int
%hd,ho,hx	integer in decimal, octal or hexadecimal form to short int

Not all compilers provide every one of these conversions, and some provide more, so check your language reference manual if you are going to do any sophisticated input.

The scanf() allows us to specify the maximum size of an incoming field. The scanf() will keep getting input until this maximum width has been reached or white space has been encountered. Regardless of what caused the conversion to stop, the next conversion will pick up wherever the last input finished. White space is skipped because it is usually used to separate input. In the special case of character input, white space will not be skipped. This is especially useful for entering strings that might contain white space such as blanks. By specifying the maximum width, we can accept strings of a fixed length. (Always make your character array one larger than the real string to hold the special termination character.) An example is shown below.

```
char message[21];
scanf("%20c", message);
```

One of the more common needs in input processing is to get the next non-white space character. This can't be done easily with '%c' because it doesn't

it is to use '%1s', which ignores all
~acter and has a field width of 1.
￢ful formatting capabilities, it
┘e. Look at the code below.

.ess loop if the user inputs an alphabetic char-
┘he '-'). When a `scanf()` conversion is un-
↗' the characters to the keyboard. In this case, be-
in a loop it will immediately get the improper data

˄cter Input and Output

┘e your own input routines by using `getchar()`. `getchar()`
┘ingle character from the keyboard into an integer type value. You
┘use an integer for the return variable because the common end-of-file
┘acter cannot be represented by 'char' type data on some machines.
┘etchar() returns the next character available from the keyboard including
carriage returns, tabs, and other control characters. The following code gets
data from the keyboard and puts it to the screen using `putchar()`.

```
int c;
do
   {  c = getchar();
      putchar(c);
   } while( c != '\n' );
```

`putchar()` is used to put single characters to the screen. You must
provide `putchar()` with either a character literal, which is enclosed in
single quotes (e.g., `putchar('H');`) or an integer or character variable
name. The last two lines of the code below produce exactly the same output.

```
int  c = 72, d = 73;   /* ASCII codes for 'H' and 'I' */

putchar(c); putchar(d); putchar('\n');
putchar('H'); putchar('I'); putchar('\n');
```

THE SWITCH

It is fairly common to have situations in which a variable can take on several
different values, and each different value requires a different action to be performed. An example could be actions that depend on codes. We could solve
this problem by using an `if...else` structure but the best way is to use a
`switch`. The `switch` allows you to list all the cases you wish to act on and
then describe the action that depends on each case. The 'lotto' program is a
simple illustration, where we must assign different winnings for different
numbers of correct digits.

```
main()
{  int correct_digits;
   float winnings;


   scanf("%d", &correct_digits);


   switch(correct_digits)
   {  case  5: winnings = 1000000.00;
               break;
      case  4: winnings = 10000.00;
               break;
      case  3: winnings = 100.00;
               break;
      default: winnings = 0.00;
               break;
   }
   printf("you have won %f in this lottery\n", winnings);
}
```

We can use switches only with variables that have discrete values (integers and characters) such as 'correct_digits'. We describe each case that we wish to deal with individually. When that case occurs, the code following the ':' is executed until it hits the end of the switch or the first break occurs.

NOTE: We had to place breaks in the code to prevent the program from falling through from one case into another. You can describe a default action if none of the other cases have been satisfied.

In some cases the same action must be performed for several different cases. For example, if we had to determine the length of a month depending on the month number, several have 31 days, several have 30 days, and February has 28 or 29 days. We can get around this by lining up all the cases that require the same action, and put the break only after the last case in the group. The following code illustrates this point.

```
/* Simple program illustrating the 'switch'. */

#define FOREVER 1
#define QUIT 99

main()
{ int month;

   while ( FOREVER )
   {
       printf(" input month number or  99 to quit\n");
       scanf("%d", &month);
       if ( month == QUIT ) break;
```

```
        switch(month)
        { case 1:
          case 3:
          case 5:
          case 7:
          case 8:
          case 10:
          case 12: printf("month has 31 days\n");
                   break;
          case 4:
          case 6:
          case 9:
          case 11: printf("month has 30 days\n");
                   break;
          case 2:  printf("February has 28 days,\n");
                   printf("29 days on a leap year\n");
                   break;
          default: printf("improper month number \n");
                   break;
        }
    }
}
```

ALTERING CONTROL

There are three instructions that can be used to alter the way our code will execute: goto, break, and continue. All three instructions should be avoided if possible because they tend to cause debugging problems. The goto is of special interest. The irresponsible use of gotos and the software system disasters they helped cause were among the reasons for the original development of structured programming techniques. The main problem with gotos is that if they are used indiscriminately it will be almost impossible to trace the paths of control, and therefore impossible to estimate the 'state' of your program (i.e., the variable contents) at any time. The continue, break, and goto can usually be avoided by the proper use of structured loops and structured ifs.

The goto causes control to jump directly to a label. A label is simply a name given to a particular location in a program. In C, you create a label by placing a ':' after a valid C name. You are allowed only to goto a label in the same function as the goto. An example of the use of a goto and labels is shown below.

```
int x;

if ( x <= 21 )
    goto sloppy_code;

  /* this area would contain code to be executed when
     x is greater than 21   */

sloppy_code:
/* this code would be executed when x is less than or
     equal to 21   */
```

The continue is used inside loops. It will cause the next iteration of a loop to start immediately, regardless of how many statements lie between the continue and the bottom of the loop. In the special case of using a continue within a `for` loop, the counters will be incremented or decremented and the condition checked before the next iteration starts.

The `break` causes a proper exit out of the closest loop or `switch`. It is used more commonly than the `continue`. It is typically used with those looping conditions that are awkward to place at the top or the bottom of a loop. In addition, sometimes the main conditions for looping can be placed at the top or bottom but some special event can occur somewhere in the middle of the loop that requires an immediate exit. Because programmers typically look at the top or bottom of a loop for the exit conditions, the `break` can cause some debugging problems. One solution might be to label any `break` with comment code.

One possible use for the `continue` and the `break` is for any complex data input process. Interactive programs commonly get screenfuls of data using screen input forms. A person entering the data might determine midway through a screen that the entire screen of data is questionable and wish to continue immediately with the next set of data, or quit the inputting routine entirely. The `continue` and the `break` are perfect for this task. The following code accepts payroll information from a user (employee number, hours worked, and hourly rate) and allows him or her to cancel or quit at any entry. Assume that special functions to get, clear, and save the data have already been written. The proper creation and use of these user-written functions will be discussed in Chapter 4.

```c
#define FOREVER 1
#define QUIT -99
#define CANCEL -80

int id_no;
float hours, rate;

while ( FOREVER )
{
  clear_input_fields();
  id_no = get_id();
  if ( id_no == QUIT )
     break;                      /**** LOOP EXIT ****/
  else if ( id_no == CANCEL )
     continue;

  hours = get_hours();
  if ( hours == QUIT )
     break;                      /**** LOOP EXIT ****/
  else if ( hours == CANCEL )
     continue;

  rate = get_rate();
  if ( rate == QUIT )
     break;                      /**** LOOP EXIT ****/
  else if ( rate == CANCEL )
     continue;

  save_data();
}
```

PUTTING IT TOGETHER

COMMODITIES ENHANCEMENT 1

The following program is an enhancement of the commodities program from Chapter 1. It uses some of the features of C discussed in this chapter. This program will display the value of a commodity (gold, silver, or platinum) based on the commodity type and the amount. The whole process is put in a loop that will exit when the user enters -99 for commodity type. Both commodity type and amount are validated at input using a do...while loop. Some of the more important features of the code are discussed below.

Using '#define'
Using #define will help make our program more readable and more easily modified later on. If we had to change the actual gold or silver rate later on, we would have to change only the two #define statements at the top of the program and not search through the entire code for any 450.00 and 7.00.

Using Loops
We have used two types of loops here, a while and a do...while. The while is an endless loop (FOREVER is always true) so that we must break somewhere inside the loop using a break. A do...while was used for our input validation because we needed to go through the loop at least once before we performed our test for an exit condition.

Using 'switch'
We used the switch to test the commodity type because we were testing several discrete values of a single integer type variable.

Using 'break'
We used an if with a break to exit our main loop. Because programmers typically expect to find exit conditions at the top or bottom of a loop, we have labeled the exit with comment code.

Using Special Formatting with 'printf()'
We specified that our value be displayed with a minimum field size of ten and that the result should be rounded to two decimal places. The conversion specification for this was '%10.2f'.

```c
/* COMMOD1.C  This program will display the value of a
              commodity based on the type and amount. Both type
              and amount are validated to see that they are within
              range. Language features used include #define,
              do..while, break, switch, and formatting of output */

#include <stdio.h>
#define GOLD 1
#define SILVER 2
#define PLATINUM 3
#define GOLD_RATE 450.00
#define SILVER_RATE 7.00
#define PLAT_RATE 600.00
#define FOREVER 1
#define QUIT -99
```

```
main()
{
    int type;
    float amount;
    float total_value;
    while ( FOREVER )
    {
      do{
          printf("\n\t%d  Gold", GOLD);
          printf("\n\t%d  Silver", SILVER);
          printf("\n\t%d  Platinum", PLATINUM);
          printf("\n\t%d QUIT\n", QUIT);
          printf("\nEnter Type of Commodity: ");
          scanf("%d", &type);
        } while ( type != QUIT  && type != GOLD
                && type != PLATINUM && type != SILVER ) ;

      if ( type == QUIT ) break;              /**** LOOP EXIT ****/

      do{
          printf("\nEnter number of ounces: ");
          scanf("%f", &amount);
        } while ( amount < 0.0 );

      switch ( type )
      {   case GOLD     : total_value = GOLD_RATE * amount;
                          break;
          case SILVER   : total_value = SILVER_RATE * amount;
                          break;
          case PLATINUM: total_value = PLAT_RATE * amount;
                          break;
      }
      printf("The total value for your metal is %10.2f\n",
                total_value);
    }
}
```

LABORATORY 2

1. Experiment with assignments by assigning a variety of numbers to signed and unsigned, and long and normal integers.

2. Write a program, using the sizeof() function and printf(), to display the length of each data type on your machine.

3. What is displayed by the following code?
```
int street_no = 123;
static char street_name[20] = "Lakeshore Rd.";
float num = 1234.5678;

printf("%04d***%-8.6s\n", street_no, street_name);
printf("%6.1f  %4.3f\n", num, num);
```

4. Given the following code:

```
int a = 3, b = 7, c = 23;

if ( c == 23 || b < 1 && !( a == 1 ))        printf("true\n");
if ( (c == 23 || b < 1 ) && !( a == 1 ))     printf("true\n");
if ( !( a = 17 ) && c == 23 )                printf("true\n");
if ( x = 3 * b - 7 * a )                     printf("true\n");
if ( x = 3 * b - 7 * a == 0 )                printf("true\n");
```

how many times is "true" printed? List the statements that do and do not print a message and explain why in each case.

5. Write a program that accepts an hour (integer), a minute (integer), a second (integer), and an integer representing morning or afternoon (0 if it is morning and a 1 if it is the afternoon). Calculate and print out the number of seconds from midnight to the time that was entered.

6. Going along Main Street, the lights on First Avenue, Second Avenue, Third Avenue, and Fourth Avenue are exactly 7 seconds apart. Every green light lasts for 25 seconds, every yellow light lasts 6 seconds, and every red light lasts 25 seconds. If the green light on First Avenue started at exactly 12:00 midnight, what color is the stoplight at Third Avenue, at 3:15:43 on the following afternoon? For a refinement, allow the user to enter any time and any light, and display the color of the light.

3

THE ARRAY

As in other languages, C allows the programmer to group elements of similar size and type into an array. The syntax for declaring an array is shown below.

```
int    valid_codes[40];
```

Data type of individual element

Array name

Number of elements

As you can see, the data type of the individual element must be specified first and in C, we use square brackets, not round, when dealing with arrays. Another interesting feature of C is that, although we specified 40 elements in 'valid_codes', the elements would be numbered starting at 0, and ending at 39 (not 40). Be careful of this point. The example below compares a code that has been entered against an array of valid codes. It will break out of the loop when it has gone through all 40 codes or when a match has occurred. Notice that our loop has a null body. We do not need any statements inside this loop because all the necessary conditions for our search are contained in the `for` conditions themselves.

```
#include MAX_CODES   40

int count, in_code, valid_codes[MAX_CODES];

scanf("%d", &in_code);
for ( count = 0;
      count < MAX_CODES  &&  in_code != valid_codes[count];
      count++ )
      ;                   /* NULL BODY  */

if ( count < MAX_CODES )
    printf("your code is valid\n");
```

We can use arrays to store any fixed size element, whether it is an integer, a long integer, a float, characters, other arrays, or the structures and pointers that we will learn about later on. Perhaps the most important type of array is the character array, which we will use to store strings such as messages and names. We can process strings in the same way we process arrays or by using one of several string-processing functions in the standard library. Look at the declarations below. Pay special note to the two-dimensional array (the elements in that array would be numbered from 'two_d[0][0]' to 'two_d[5][4]').

```
long int big_n[30];
char name[25];
float two_d[6][5];
```

Strings as Arrays

Because strings (e.g., names, messages) are so important in so many programs, we will devote an entire chapter to string processing later on. However, since strings are little more than arrays of characters, the concepts we learn here about array processing can be used in string processing.

Initializing Arrays

You will often want to set initial values for an array. You can do this by providing an initializer list in braces (curly brackets). Declaring the array as `static` will ensure that if you provide fewer initializers than the size of the array, the remaining values will default to zero if it is a numeric variable and null if it is a character. The keyword `static` is discussed in the next chapter.

```
static int fibnumbers[6] = { 1, 1, 2, 3, 5, 8 };
```

If we provide an initializer list, we don't have to specify how many elements are in our array. It will default to the number of initializers.

```
static int fibnumber[] = { 1, 1, 2, 3, 5, 8 };
```

Initializing a two-dimensional array is similar to initializing one-dimensional arrays, but here you can nest the braces to represent the repeating groups. For instance, a four-by-three array of long integers is really four repeating groups of three long integers. An example is found below.

```
static long int bignumbers[4][3] = { {1000L, 2000L, 3000L},
                                      {1L, 2L, 3L},
                                      {10L},
                                      {100L, 200L}
                                    };
```

You should see four different groups enclosed in braces—they correspond to rows. The array definition says that each row has three elements, but only one or two elements have been initialized in two rows. In those cases the remaining elements in that row are assigned the value 0.

PUTTING IT TOGETHER

COMMODITIES ENHANCEMENT 2

We will enhance the commodities program from Chapter 2 by adding more commodities and by using an array instead of a `switch` to select the proper commodity price. Although we added six more options, the code is shorter and in many ways simpler. We use the actual commodity type value to select the element in our 'price' array. This is done in our `printf()` statement. We declared an array of `float` type data to hold our prices. We did not have to specify the number of elements, because C will automatically reserve enough elements when you provide an initializer list. Our initializer list was enclosed in braces. Because array elements are numbered starting from zero, we had to put an extra 0.0 in the array, so that element 1 (gold) would correspond to 450.00, element 2 would be 7.00, etc.

```
/*   COMMOD2.C  This is a conversion of COMMOD1.C to use an
               array of prices instead of using #define's.
               The code is shorter and less complex. */

#include <stdio.h>
#define HIGH_VALUE 9
#define LOW_VALUE 1
#define FOREVER 1
#define QUIT -99

main()
{
    int type;
    float amount;
    float total_value;

    static float prices[]= { 0.0, 450.00,    7.00, 600.00,
                                   14.90,    1.30,    2.00,
                                    4.50, 110.00,    8.00
                           };

    while ( FOREVER )
    {
      do{
          printf("\n01 GOLD     \t04 OIL       \t07 WHEAT");
          printf("\n02 SILVER   \t05 ALUMINUM \t08 BEEF");
          printf("\n03 PLATINUM \t06 COPPER    \t09 SOYBEANS");
          printf("\nSelect one of the above or %d to QUIT :",
                  QUIT);
          scanf("%d", &type);
        } while ( type != QUIT &&
                  ( type < LOW_VALUE || type > HIGH_VALUE ) );

      if ( type == QUIT ) break;                 /**** LOOP EXIT ****/

      do{
          printf("\nEnter number of ounces: ");
          scanf("%f", &amount);
        } while ( amount < 0.0 );

      printf("The total value for your metal is %10.2f\n",
              prices[type] * amount);
    }
}
```

LABORATORY 3

1. Initialize an array of integers with the length of each month. Allow a user to inquire about the length of any month. (Don't worry about leap years.)

2. Write a program that accepts five numbers (floating point) representing the daily closing prices of a stock for a week. Find the highest one-day and two-day changes in the stock price over that week and print out the results.

3. A Julian date is the number of days since the beginning of the year (i.e., January 1 is 1, and December 31 is 365). Have a user enter the month and day, and display the Julian date. (Don't worry about leap years.)

4. Write a program that will check a five-element array of integers for duplicates (i.e., pairs). Have a user enter numbers into the array.

5. Write a program that will go through every possible combination of rolls for two dice starting at 1,1 and going to 6,6, and count how many times a particular total comes up (i.e., how many 2's, how many 7's, etc.). Print out the results for each total. For a refinement, also print out the probability of a particular roll coming up.

6. We have a five-by-five pricing grid for different qualities of gems. Prices should increase from right to left in each row, and from top to bottom in each column. Write a program to validate this pricing array, saving the positions that are possibly incorrect in a separate array.

4

FUNCTIONS AND STORAGE CLASSES

C provides several facilities for the implementation of structured design techniques. The two features we will use for this are the 'function', and the proper use of storage classes. A complete treatment of structured design techniques is beyond the scope of this workbook, so we will briefly look at a few major design considerations, then concentrate on how to code a good structured design. Our shortened list of design considerations is shown below.

1. Break the job into modules using functions.
2. Set up your functions as black boxes wherever possible.
3. Use local instead of global variables wherever possible.

A black box is any object which, when given specified inputs, will give a prescribed output. You should not have to know anything about the internal workings of a black box in order to use it effectively. It should also have no side-effects such as setting variables that occur elsewhere in the program.

We will look at building robust programs by using functions. Although there are several language features that must be learned to create and use functions, two concepts in function use are especially important:

1. Understanding how to make functions communicate with one another.
2. Building functions so that they are relatively independent and safely protected from the activities of other functions.

FUNCTIONS

Functions are named blocks of code that will be executed by simply using their names (this is called invoking a function). They are usually designed to carry out a specific task. We have already seen the `printf()` and `scanf()` functions that were used to perform our printing and data input tasks.

For a function to work properly it might require that we send it data necessary to do the task, and the function in response might have some data to return to the statement that called it. To illustrate this we will take a closer look at the `scanf()` function that we used in earlier chapters. An example of the `scanf()` is shown below.

```
int num;
scanf("%d", &num);
```

We have caused the `scanf()` to perform its task just by using its name in a statement. It will take information entered at the keyboard, do an appropriate conversion to the right data type, then deposit the number in a variable. This function requires some information from the calling statement to complete its task. In this case, it needs a conversion string first ("%d"), to know what type of conversion to perform, and the location of a variable (&num) to know where to deposit the number.

Sometimes functions will return information that can be used by the calling statement. For instance, `scanf()` will return an integer representing the number of successful conversions it made. In this case, the `scanf()` will return a 1 if it was successful in converting the keyboard input into an integer (i.e., data entered was numeric). The code below shows how this returned value could be used.

```
int conversions, num;
printf("enter an integer\n");
conversions = scanf("%d", &num);
if ( conversions == 1 )
    printf("your number is %d\n", num);
else
    printf("could not convert the data as entered\n");
```

As you can see, the `scanf()` returned an integer and we assigned that value to a variable, 'conversions'. We could have used the return value (or the function itself) in the same way we used any integer in C.

Now we will look at building and using our own functions. This is the process of defining a function. We will have to describe everything from the type of data the function receives to the actual code necessary to perform its task. To define our own functions we need the following facilities:

- Mechanism to name the function.
- Mechanism to define the data type of the return value (and therefore the type of the function).
- Mechanism to receive data from the caller and to define the data that is received.
- Mechanism to return data to a caller (if necessary).
- Mechanism to define the procedure to be executed.

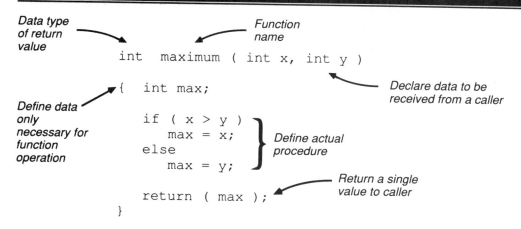

```
int  maximum ( int x, int y )

{  int max;

   if ( x > y )
      max = x;
   else
      max = y;

   return ( max );
}
```

Once the function is defined, we could use it as shown below to find the higher value of any two integer values sent to it. These integers may be either variables or constants.

```
int   high1, high2, a = 3, b = 1, c = 27;

high1 = maximum(a, b);
high2 = maximum(c, 21);
```

The examples above conform to the ANSI standard for defining functions. Some of the older compilers allow you only to specify the data names of data being received in the opening parentheses. You must declare the types of these data items immediately after the closing parenthesis, and before the opening brace of the function. The changes are minor. An example of the 'maximum()' function coded in 'old' C is shown below. Notice where and how data items 'x' and 'y' are declared.

```
int maximum( x, y )
int x;
int y;
{
    int max;
    if ( x > y )
        max = x;
    else
        max = y;

    return ( max );
}
```

There are some special things to consider when using functions. First, once a function has been defined you must always send data down to it in the same order it receives it. Second, a function should be declared or defined somewhere in your program before it is ever used in a statement (i.e., called); otherwise, C will assume the function is an integer function.

In our function definition we went through a process of defining everything from the parameters sent down to the statements necessary to perform the task. A function declaration or prototype simply tells the compiler what type of data is to be returned and what type of data is to be sent down (parameters) to the function. An example of a function declaration is shown below.

```
float f1( int q,  double r );
```

This lets the compiler know that any time the function 'f1( )' is used in a statement to expect a float being returned, regardless if the function definition has been encountered or not, and that the first argument should always be an integer and the second one a double. In other words, it helps the compiler check that the function is called properly throughout our program. The parameter names above are optional but they should be used to enhance the clarity of the code. The following code is legal and is the equivalent of the above:

```
float f1( int, double );
```

Both function declarations and function prototypes are commonly placed at the top of programs, outside of the `main()`. In 'old' C you were not allowed to specify the data types of the parameters in a declaration. It meant less work for the programmer but also less safety. Since it was considered a major weakness in the original language definition, the addition of prototypes to ANSI C is considered one of the most important changes. In order to declare a function in 'old' C, you had only to provide the return data type and the function name. The following code illustrates how 'f1' would be declared in older compilers.

```
float f1();
```

There will be many cases in which you will write a function that will not return any value. This is comparable to writing a procedure in other languages. A special data type has been developed to handle this situation, `void`. Declaring a function `void` means that the function doesn't return a value. The compiler will check to ensure that the function code does not return a value and that a return value is not used in the calling statement. `void` can also be used to specify that a function will not receive any data items from the caller. By placing a `void` inside the opening parentheses of the function definition, the compiler will check that the function is never called improperly (i.e., data being sent down). Although `void` is part of the ANSI standard, it might not be available on some older compilers. An example of the use of `void` in a function definition is shown below.

```
void f1( void )
{
  printf("this function doesn't receive ");
  printf("or return any data\n");
}
```

WRITING A PROGRAM USING FUNCTIONS

Let's see if we can use what we've learned up to this point to write a simple, structured program using functions. Our main concern is to design our program by factoring our job into smaller tasks, and encode these tasks in functions. Every function should perform one well-defined task. We should also watch out for functions that can be used in other programs, so that we may set up a library of tools (commonly used functions).

The application we will use is simple—we will write a program to calculate the net cost of buying stocks, including the commission costs. Most brokers have a formula for charging commission that considers both the cost of an individual share and the total size of the transaction.

Level 0
> do while user wishes to continue
>> get number of shares, and stock price
>> calculate principal amount
>>> (code as a function 'prncpl_amt')
>> calculate commission cost
>>> (code as a function 'commission')
>> calculate net cost
>> print out results for net cost and commissions

Level 1
> 'prncpl_amt'
>> calculate principal amount by
>>> principal = number of shares * share price

> 'commission'
>> if principal amount is less than the minimum amount
>>> charge the minimum commission
>> otherwise
>>> search commission table to find correct bracket
>>>> and commission per share
>>> calculate commission from minimum commission
>>>> plus number of shares times commission per share

```c
#include <stdio.h>
#define   MIN_CHARGE 30.00
#define   MIN_BASE 2000.00
#define   FOREVER 1
#define   QUIT -99

float commission( int shares, float base, float st_price );
float prncpl_amt( int shares, float cost );

float com_rate[5][2] ={ { 30.00, .06 },
                        { 20.00, .05 },
                        { 10.00, .04 },
                        {  5.00, .03 },
                        {  0.00, .02 }};
main()
{ float price, base_cost, com_cost, net_cost;
  int no_shares;

  while(FOREVER)
  {
    printf("\ninput no. of shares (%d to quit)", QUIT);
    scanf("%d", &no_shares);
    if ( no_shares ==  QUIT )
            break;                  /**** LOOP EXIT ****/
    printf("\ninput share price  ");
    scanf("%f", &price);
```

```
            base_cost = prncpl_amt(no_shares, price);
            com_cost  = commission(no_shares, base_cost, price);
            net_cost  = base_cost + com_cost;

            printf("your net cost for %d shares at %f is %f\n",
                               no_shares, price, net_cost);
            printf("your commission cost is %f\n", com_cost);
        }
    }

float commission( int shares, float base, float st_price )
{
    int i, result;

    result = MIN_CHARGE;
    if ( base > MIN_BASE )
    {
      for ( i=0; st_price > com_rate[i][0]; i++ )
            ;              /*  NULL BODY  */
      result +=  shares * com_rate[i][1];
    }
    return ( result );
}

float prncpl_amt( int shares, float cost )
{
  return ( cost * shares );
}
```

There are a few things we can look at in the code above.

Function Design

We should already know what task must be performed from our gross design. Decide what pieces of data are necessary to complete the task, and what type of data should be returned. For example:

* Both 'commission' and 'prncpl_amt' must be of type float because they must return decimal values.

* 'commission' needs a value for the number of shares, a value for the price of the shares, and a value for the principal amount, to perform its task properly. The share price and principal amount will be of type `float`, and the number of shares will be an integer.

* 'prncpl_amt' needs a value for the number of shares and a value for the price of shares to perform its task properly. The number of shares will be an integer (it will always be a whole number), and the price will be a `float` (it might have a fractional part).

Sending Data to Functions

* Always send data to a function in the order specified in the function definition. Therefore for 'prncpl_amt', we must always send a value for number of shares first, and a value for share price second.

Prototyping

- We provided prototypes for both 'commission' and 'prncpl_amt' at the top of the program. These inform the compiler of the expected return data types and expected parameter data types for both functions.

Null-bodied Loop

- The `for` loop in the 'commission' function has a null or empty statement. The only task necessary for our search is to increment the counter until our stock price is in the right commission bracket. All of this work can be done within the statements of the `for` loop. Always comment Null bodies so that they will not be overlooked.

USING ARRAYS WITH FUNCTIONS

We might want to create generalized functions to process different arrays. We can send down the location of an array or part of an array. This doesn't send down every value in the array to the function. It tells the called function where to find the data in the calling function.

We will create a function that returns the highest value of various floating point arrays. This could mean a four-element single-dimension array or a five-element row in a two-dimension array. Please notice that in order to send a single dimension four-element array we could just name it (rates). To send a row in a two-dimension array we can use the 'address of' operator '&' and the first element in that row (i.e., &numbers[1][0]). In our function 'highest' we will receive a count of the elements in the array as an integer, and then the array itself.

```
float highest( int count, float array[] );

main()
{
    float highest_rate, highest_in_second;
    static float rates[] = { .095, .0875, .099, .088 };

    static float numbers[][] = {
                                { 25.3, 15.2, 56.2, 9.7, 14.5 },
                                { 15.2, .4, 7.1, 234.8, .89 },
                                { 16.8, 28.1 }
                               };

    highest_rate = highest(4, rates);
    highest_in_second = highest(5, &(numbers[1][0]));
    printf("highest rate is %f\n", highest_rate);
    printf("high value in second row is %f\n", highest_in_second);
}
```

```
float highest( int count, float array[] )
{
    int i;
    float high;

    high = array[0];
    for( i = 1; i < count; i++ )
       if( array[i] > high )
          high = array[i];

    return ( high );
}
```

PROGRAMS, FUNCTIONS, AND CLASSES OF VARIABLES

We have just looked at how to factor a job into smaller tasks or modules by using functions. This feature alone is not enough to create robust structured programs. We must also have methods to share data among the functions, and to protect the data inside functions from accidental alteration by other modules.

The method to share data among programs without passing them is by declaring a global variable. Any time a variable is declared outside of any function, it is visible and can be used by all statements below it in the program. For this reason, global variables are often declared at the top of the program. The problem with global variables is that because they are visible to the whole program (or file), they can be accidentally altered by any of the functions. This could make debugging very difficult. Globals are sometimes necessary for messy situations when the same piece of data is to be used by several modules, perhaps at different levels of the program hierarchy. Always try to keep the use of global variables to a minimum.

In C, a program may be composed of several different parts called 'source files', each of which can be compiled separately and later linked together to form the program. To access a global variable on another source file, you must precede it with the keyword `extern`. This simply tells the compiler to look for a variable definition under that name in another file instead of creating it anew. If you are declaring external arrays, you don't have to declare the size of the first dimension (e.g., extern int two [][3];).

In addition to declaring external variables you can also declare external functions. Once again, if you declare a function as `extern` it simply means that the function is defined in a separate source file. All function declarations default to `extern`. An example of an external function definition is shown below.

```
extern int f1( double q, int r );
```

In some cases we might want to create global variables or functions that are accessible only to the file in which they occur. This often results in safer code. In order to do this, simply precede the global variable definition or function definition with the keyword `static`.

A simple example of a program that consists of two files and uses both static and external globals is shown below.

```
/* FILE1.C  This program contains two variables. It can be
            compiled separately from FILE2.C   */

int this_is_global = 200;
static int only_visible_in_file1 = 45;
extern void f2( void );
main()
{
    printf(" in file1, global %d, static global %d\n",
                    this_is_global, only_visible_in_file1);
    f2();
}
/* END OF PROGRAM FILE 1*/

---------------------------------------------------------------

/* FILE2.C  This program simply prints out the value of a global
            in file 1    */

extern int this_is_global;

void f2( void )
{       printf(" the value of the global in file 1 is %d\n",
                    this_is_global);
}
/* END OF PROGRAM FILE 2*/
```

The two files above, when compiled separately, then linked and run will just print out the values of the global data in the first file. Try altering file 2 to print out the value of the static global in file 1. It should cause an error.

An important feature of good program design is information hiding. Simply put, this means that if a piece of data is visible only to a small part of a program, there is little or no chance that the rest of the program can accidentally alter that data. This is achieved in C by using local variables, which are visible only in the functions in which they are used. Any variable declared inside a function is visible only within that function. Most of the variables we have used to this point have been local to `main()` or to one of our other functions.

There are two types of local variables: automatic and static. Automatic variables are created and destroyed with every call to the function that contains them. This means that they will lose their values between function calls. Automatic variables are the default class, although you can declare them explicitly by using the keyword `auto`. If you want your local variables to retain their values between function calls, you must precede their definition with the keyword `static`.

The program below illustrates some features of global, automatic, and static variables. WHAT IS PRINTED?

```
    int x = 5;                           /* global variable declared outside
                                            of any function                  */

    int f1( void ), f2( void ), f3( void );    /* function prototypes */

    main()
    {
        int i;
        int p, q, r;
        for ( i = 1 ;i <= 5 ; i++ )          /* iterate each function 5 times */
        {
            p = f1();
            q = f2();
            r = f3();
        }
        printf(" sum using global %d\n", p);
        printf(" sum using local automatic %d\n", q);
        printf(" sum using local static %d\n", r);
    }

    int f1( void )                       /* 'f1' uses a global variable to */
    {   x += 5;                          /* sum                            */
        return x;
    }

    int f2( void )                       /*  'f2' uses the default, a local */
    {   int x = 0;                       /*  automatic to sum               */
        x += 5;
        return x;
    }

    int f3( void )                       /*  'f3' uses a local static to    */
    {   static int x = 0;                /*  sum                            */
        x += 5;
        return x;
    }
```

The program above uses both global and local variables, and automatic and static variables.

The only global variable in the program is the 'x' at the top of the page. It is a global variable because it has been defined outside of any functions. It can be accessed from within any of the functions that are defined below it. The global 'x' is used in the function 'f1()'. All global variables remain alive throughout the program run. It is initialized with a value of 5 and we add 5 five times so its final value is 30.

Two of the local variables in this program are 'x' in the function 'f2()', and 'x' in the function 'f3()'. They are two separate variables because they occur in separate functions. They are local because they were defined within a function. Since they are local, they can be accessed only from inside the function in which they were declared. Local variables take precedence over global variables if they have the same name (i.e., C ignores the global 'x' in f2() and uses the 'x' defined within the function).

In 'f2()', because we didn't specify any special storage class, 'x' defaulted to an automatic variable. This means it will be created and destroyed every time the function is called. This makes it impossible to accumulate values between calls to the function. Its final value will be 5.

In 'f3()', we specified that 'x' should be static. This means that we want to keep the values in 'x' between function calls. Because values are preserved between function calls, when we print the final value using this function we will get 25.

FUNCTIONS—A SYNOPSIS

What Are They?

Functions are a named unit of a program that will execute just by using its name in a statement. When a function completes execution, control automatically returns to the statement that called it.

What Are They Used For?

They allow us to subdivide a program into smaller units that are more easily coded and debugged. They also give the ability to hide data inside a function from the rest of the program.

How Do You Define a Function?

To define a function you must provide the following:

1. A name.
2. Data type of the return value.
3. Description of any parameters sent down.
4. Declaration of private variables.
5. Necessary code to complete the task.
6. If necessary, a statement to return data to the caller.

How Do You Declare a Function?

Declaring a function is simply telling the compiler what type of return value to expect if the compiler hasn't seen its definition yet. ANSI compilers also allow you to specify the data type of each of the parameters sent down. This enhances safety by letting the compiler check that you have been consistent in your use of the function. It takes the following form.

```
float float_fn( int x, float y, int z );
```

With older compilers you may not be able to specify the data types of the parameters. In this case the function declarations look as below:

```
float float_fn();
```

STORAGE CLASSES—A SYNOPSIS

What Are They?

Storage classes indicate how a data object will be stored. This will control how long the variable is active and how much of the program will be able to access the variable.

What Are They Used For?

They allow the programmer to control how any variable is either hidden or shared within a program. The fewer statements that are allowed to access a variable, the less chance of accidental alteration. Storage classes also help to use memory more efficiently since the memory used by automatic variables is released after a function has completed execution.

How Do You Control Visibility (Scope)?

Any variable declared inside a function is considered a local variable, that is, it can be accessed only by statements inside the same function.

Any variable defined outside of any function is considered global and can be accessed from anywhere within the file. To access a global variable that was defined in another source file, you must precede your declaration with `extern`. You can restrict access to a global variable by preceding it with `static`. This will restrict access to only the statements in the same file in which it was defined.

How Do You Control Duration (Longevity)?

All global variables remain active throughout the entire program run.

All local variables default to automatic variables unless you precede their definition with `static`. Automatic variables remain active only during the execution of the function. They will lose their values after the function has completed execution. To make a local variable remain active throughout the program run, precede its definition by the keyword `static`.

PUTTING IT TOGETHER

COMMODITIES ENHANCEMENT 3

We are now ready to build a program composed of several functions on several different source files. These source files will be compiled separately then linked into one executable or runnable file. The source files will be set up so that the functions and data declared within them contribute to the same general task. We will have one source file for our driver, "commod3.c", one source file that will get and validate any necessary data, "c3_data.c", and one source file to determine the commodity price, "c3_price.c" and a header file for commonly used definitions, "commod3.h". In the case of "c3_price.c" it might seem like overkill to have one source file for one function, but this could be the source file that must be changed the most. The number of commodities might increase, a more flexible search method might be required, or we might have to load the array of prices from a file. Always try to look ahead when you allocate functions and tasks to source files.

In "commod3.c" you should note that the code for the driver is less complex because we have moved much of the work to lower level functions. We were required to prototype the functions from the other files before we could call them. These functions did all the work of getting both the amount and commodity type. We always tested the return value for a QUIT instruction. The return value from 'price()' was used to calculate a price. 'price()' returns an error code of -1 if it is not able to calculate a price. It is a good idea to write functions so that they return error codes, and that your code test for these values.

In 'price()' we simply took the code to determine a price from "commod2.c" and rewrote it as a function. It receives an integer representing the commodity, checks that it is within range, and either returns the price or an error code depending on whether the commodity type was correct.

In "c3_data.c" we have put all the functions necessary to get and validate any necessary data. Once again, we essentially took the code from "commod2.c" and rewrote them as functions. Although 'valid_code()' looks like a trivial function, validations can often grow more complex over the life of a project, so we encoded this task as a separate function.

An interesting feature of this type of design is that 'management' occurs at the top level of the program (the driver) and real work occurs further down. This can help make `main()` much more easily understood.

```
/* COMMOD3.H   Header file for Commodity program */
#define TRUE 1
#define FALSE 0
#define QUIT -99
#define HIGH_VALUE 9
#define LOW_VALUE 4


------------------------------------------------------------------
/* COMMOD3.C  This is the driver for a program which gets
              a commodity type and amount and prints out the total
              value. It must call functions in c3_price.c and
              c3_data.c                                          */

#include <stdio.h>
#include "commod3.h"

float get_price( int commodity );
float get_amount( void ) ;
int get_commodity( void );

main()
{   int commod;
    float amount;
    float price;
    float total_value;

    while ( FOREVER )
    { commod = get_commodity();
      if( commod == QUIT) break;                  /**** LOOP EXIT ****/
      amount = get_amount();
      if( amount == QUIT) break;                  /**** LOOP EXIT ****/

      if ( (price = get_price( commod )) > 0.0 )
         printf("The total value for your commodity is %10.2f\n",
                 price * amount );
      else
         printf("Invalid commodity code\n");
    }
}

------------------------------------------------------------------
```

```
/* C3_PRICE.C  This file contains a function to generate prices
               based on a commodity code (get_price).            */

#include "commod3.h"
int valid_code( int code );

float get_price( int commodity )
{
    static int prices[]= { 0.0,  450.00,   7.00, 600.00,
                                    .60,     .30,   2.00,
                                  20.00,   40.00,  23.00
                         };
    if ( valid_code( commodity ) )
        return ( prices[commodity] );
    else
        return ( -1 );
}
------------------------------------------------------------------

/*  C3_DATA.C  This file will get any necessary data for the Commodity
               system. It contains functions to get and validate
               the commodity type and one to get the amount.      */

#include <stdio.h>
#include "commod3.h"

int get_commodity( void )
{   int commodity;
    int valid = FALSE;

    printf("\n01 GOLD    \t04 OIL     \t07 WHEAT");
    printf("\n02 SILVER  \t05 ALUMINUM\t08 BEEF");
    printf("\n03 PLATINUM\t06 COPPER  \t09 SOYBEANS");
    printf("\nSelect one of the above or %d to QUIT:",
            QUIT);

    do{
        scanf("%d", &commodity);
        if ( valid_code(commodity) != TRUE
            && commodity != QUIT )
          printf("\ninvalid commodity code");
        else
            valid = TRUE;
      } while ( valid == FALSE );
    return ( commodity );
}

float get_amount( void )
{   float amount;
    int valid = FALSE;
```

```
    printf("\nEnter commodity amount or %d to QUIT",
           QUIT);
    do{
        scanf("%f", &amount);
        if ( amount <= 0.0 && amount != QUIT )
            printf("\ninvalid amount code");
        else
            valid = TRUE;
    } while ( valid == FALSE );
    return ( amount );
}

int valid_code( int code )
{   int valid = FALSE;
    if ( LOW_VALUE <= code  && code <= HIGH_VALUE )
        valid = TRUE;
    return ( valid );
}
```

LABORATORY 4

1. Write a function 'area' that calculates the area of a circle. It receives a radius (float), and returns the area (float). Test the function by calling it from `main()`.

    The formula for the area of a circle is
    area = radius * radius * 3.1459

2. Write a function 'astro( )' that receives two integers representing the month and the day, and returns an integer representing the astrological sign that date falls in. Let 1 represent Aquarius, 2 Pisces, etc. Check your local newspaper for the proper dates for each sign.

3. Create a file, "equity.c", which contains functions to perform elementary analysis on common stocks. Include the following functions.

    double p_e()—receives a stock price (double) and an earnings per share (double) and returns the price/earnings ratio (double). Price/earnings ratio is calculated by the following formula.

    price_earnings = stock_price/earnings_per_share

    double yield()—receives a stock price (double) and a stock_dividend (double) and returns the yield (double). Yield is calculated by the following formula.

    yield = stock_dividend/stock_price * 100.0

    double volume_trend()—receives yesterday's sales (long) and today's sales (long) and returns the volume trend (double). Volume trend is calculated by the following formula.

    volume trend = (todays_trades- yesterdays_trades)/ yesterdays_trades * 100.0

    Once you have written and compiled this file, create another file, "analysis.c", which will accept today's stock price, today's stock sales, yesterday's stock sales, and the stock dividend and earnings. If the p/e ratio is less than 12.0, and the yield is more than 3.0% and the volume trend is greater than -1.0%, tell the user to buy; otherwise, tell him/her to wait.

5

THE POINTER

The pointer is a special data type that allows you to store the location ("address") of data rather than the data itself. If you want to compare it to using arrays, a subscript will tell where within an array to find information, but doesn't store the actual information. Pointers will allow you to use memory more efficiently and more elegantly.

Let's take a close look at the pointer. The pointer is a data object that allows you to store the address of another data object (i.e., an integer, char, or any other data type). When a variable is declared, the compiler ensures that an area of memory large enough to hold that variable is reserved. The compiler will also ensure that the location (address) of that small memory area is available. We use pointers to access data areas by their locations or addresses instead of by name. The main things we will want to do with pointers are:

1. Set or alter the data area that the pointer points to.

2. Retrieve information from the data area that the pointer points to.

3. Alter the pointer itself, so that it points to another data area.

Like any other data type in C, we must declare a pointer before we can use it. We must state what type of object the pointer will point to, and place an '*' before the name we wish to use. For example, if we want to declare a pointer 'high' which points to an integer we would do the following:

```
int    *high;
```

Once we have declared our pointer, we will want to set and alter both the pointer and the data that the pointer points to. Whenever we wish to access a pointer, we will use the pointer name (i.e., high), and when we wish to access the data that the pointer points to we will use an '*' before our pointer name (i.e., *high). The examples on the following page illustrate the difference between a pointer and what it points to.

THE DIFFERENCE BETWEEN A POINTER AND THE OBJECT IT POINTS TO

Understanding the difference between a pointer and the object it points to is the only critical hurdle to using pointers effectively. For example, if we define a pointer as shown below, we must know the difference between using '*fpntr' and 'fpntr' in our code.

```
float *fpntr;
```

Using 'fpntr' in a statement indicates that you wish to use the pointer itself, perhaps to set it to the address of a `float`. If we wanted, we could set 'fpntr' to the address of any floating point variable, by using the "address of" operator, '&'. Below, we are setting 'fpntr' to point to the variable 'interest' by using the address operator '&' (assume that 'interest' has been defined as a `float`).

```
fpntr =  &interest;
```

'*fpntr' allows us to use or change an actual floating point number sitting at the address 'fpntr' points to. Since we have initialized 'fpntr' to point to 'interest', any reference to '*fpntr' will actually access the variable 'interest'. Now we could print out the value of 'interest' with the following statement:

```
printf("the interest on your account is %f\n", *fpntr);
```

We can use '*fpntr' exactly as we would use any `float` variable, including performing arithmetic, assignment, and printing. Once again, in the statements below, when we use '*fpntr' we are actually accessing 'interest'. The first statement changes the value of 'interest' and the second uses the value of 'interest'.

```
*fpntr = old_balance * rate;
new_balance = old_balance + *fpntr;
```

POINTER ARITHMETIC AND ARRAYS

Let's see how we could process an array of integers using pointers. Ideally, we would set a pointer to the beginning of the array and repeatedly increment the pointer up, one integer at a time, until we have finished processing all the integers. C allows us to do this using pointer arithmetic. The code below will search an array of five integers and save the address of the highest value in the array.

```
#define ELEMENTS 5
int i;
int *high, *p;
static int array[5] = { 200, 34, 78, 600, 45 };

high = p = array;

for ( i = 1; i < ELEMENTS; i++ )
{ p++;
  if ( *p > *high)
    high = p;
}
printf("the highest number is %d\n", *high);
```

We have started here by initializing our pointers to the beginning of the array. Any array name really describes the address of the first byte of the array (i.e., &array[0]).

For each iteration we would increment the pointer and compare the 'value at p' with the 'value at high'. Depending on the result, we would reset the pointer 'high'. For every loop, we had to increment the pointer 'p' by one integer, so that it would point to the next integer. We do not have to know exactly how long an integer is, in bytes; C will take care of the arithmetic for us. If an integer were actually two bytes long, and we defined a pointer to integers, incrementing that pointer by one will make it point two bytes down from the original address.

We can change our pointers by adding to or subtracting from the pointer. The first statement below would make 'p' point three integers down from the present address, and the second statement would make 'p' point to the previous integer.

```
p   += 3;
--p;
```

Now try to figure out what the following code does.

```
#define NO_ROWS 3
#define NO_COLS 4
int i, temp;
static int array[NO_ROWS][NO_COLS] = { {    1,    4,    3,    2 },
                                       {   10,   40,   30,   20 },
                                       {  100,  400,  300,  200 },
                                     };

int *p;

p = &array[0][1];

for( i = 1; i <= NO_ROWS; i++ )
{
     temp  = *p;
      *p   = *(p+2);
    *(p+2) = temp;

    p += NO_COLS;
}
```

If you guessed that it switches the second column with the fourth, you were correct. How did we do it?

Initially we set our pointer to point to the second column of row 1, (i.e., "p = &array[0][1]"). We had to use the '&' operator here, not the array name by itself, because we wanted an address somewhere inside the array.

For each loop we would swap an integer 'at p' (i.e., *p) with an integer located two integers down 'at p + 2' (i.e., *(p+2)). We swapped the values at the two locations but we did not alter the pointer 'p'.

After each loop, we must make sure the pointer points to the second element of the next row. Since each row is four integers long, if we increment the pointer by four it will automatically point to the second element of the next row.

POINTERS AND FUNCTIONS

It is often better to send pointers to functions rather than values. When swapping integers, it would be preferable if we could write a function that could swap any two integers, whether they are in a one-dimensional array, a two-dimensional array, or in two separate arrays. We can do this easily by creating a function that receives the addresses of two integers and swaps the values at those addresses.

```
void swap ( int *first, *second)
{
    int temp;
    temp = *first;
    *first = *second;
    *second = temp;
}

main()
{   int x, y, array1[20], array2[5][10];

    swap( &array[10], &array[11] );
    swap( &array2[3][4], &array2[4][4] );
    swap( &x,&y );
}
```

The 'swap' function above receives pointers to the two integers that are to be swapped. Remember that pointers are really the addresses of data, so that we must send the addresses of the data elements we wish to swap. That is why we always sent the addresses of the elements we wanted swapped, using the '&' operator.

POINTERS—A SYNOPSIS

What Are They?

A pointer is a data object that points to another data object. Pointers store the "addresses" of data objects.

What Are They Used For?

They allow us to indirectly access data. Most variable names can represent only one memory address. Pointers can represent any memory address and therefore are more flexible.

Pointers are most often used for array processing, string processing, and sending and receiving information to and from a function.

How Do You Declare a Pointer?

Specify the data type you will point to, then place a '*' before your pointer name.

```
float *fpointer;
```

What Operators Do You Use?

&: The "address" operator allows us to take the address of a variable so that we may assign it to a pointer.

```
int t, *p;
p = &t;
```

*: The 'indirection' operator placed before a pointer name tells us that we want to use the data object that the pointer points to, not the pointer itself. '*p' would be the equivalent of the integer 't' because 'p' points to 't'.

How Do You Use Them?

The only critical point in using pointers effectively is knowing the difference between a pointer and what a pointer points to. Look at the statements below.

```
float  x, *p, array[7];
p = &array[3];
p = p + 2;
*p = *p + 2;
```

The statement "p = p + 2" is altering the address in 'p' so that it points two floats down from its present position (array[3]). The statement "*p = *p + 2" adds 2 to whatever 'p' presently points to (array[5]).

LABORATORY 5

1. Using a pointer, transfer all the elements of a three-by-three array of integers called 'two_d' to a nine-element array called 'one_d'. Try copying a row at a time first, then a column at a time.

2. Using a pointer or pointers, write a program to reverse the order of a ten-element array of floating point numbers. Display the contents of the array using pointers.

3. Write a program using pointers that will switch every even-numbered element in an array of integers with its adjacent odd-numbered element (e.g., array[0] with array[1], array[2] with array[3], etc.).

4. Write a function 'shift()' that receives the starting address of a ten-element array, and an integer representing the number of elements you wish to shift to the right or left in the array. A negative integer indicates a shift to the left, and a positive integer means a shift to the right. (i.e., shift left 5 means element 6 is shifted to element 1, etc., until element 10 is shifted to element 5; all remaining elements are set to zero).

5. Using two pointers compare corresponding elements of two arrays of eight integers, 'first' and 'second', which contain only ones or zeros (binary flags). If either the element in 'first' or the element in 'second' is '0', set the element in 'first' to '0'. Print out your results.

6

STRINGS AND CHARACTERS

Although up to this point we have concentrated mostly on numeric data, it is also important that we are able to handle string data such as names, messages and text. C has a very simple definition for the string :

string: A sequence of characters terminated by a character '\0', signifying the end of the string. ('\0' is a symbol for a single character. It represents the null character.)

This simple definition is very important to the way we will handle strings. It means that if you know the address of the beginning of the string, you can set up simple loops to process the string character by character until a '\0' is reached. There is no need to know the length of the string. Because of this, all strings are identified by character array names, or character pointer names (which identify the first byte of any string).

INITIALIZING STRING ARRAYS

Since a string is a sequence of characters, we can store them in arrays of characters. When we initialize these arrays we must be sure that we include the '\0' or null character. Let's initialize a string called 'name'.

```
static char name[5] = { 'J','O','H','N','\0' };
```

We could have initialized it more easily by putting our initializing string in double quotes. C will automatically append a '\0' to the end of the characters in our double quotes, so you must be careful to leave enough room in the character array to hold the null character.

```
static char name[5] = "JOHN";
```

Two further points about initializing string arrays. First, you are allowed to leave more room in the array than necessary. Second, if you forget to include the array size, it will default to fit the size of the initializing characters plus one byte for the null character.

```
static char name[25] = "JANE DOE";
static char name[]   = "name has 18 bytes";
```

STRINGS AND POINTERS

String handling in C revolves around using the pre-defined string functions in the standard library, and customized string handling using pointers or array subscripts. We will look at the pre-defined string functions later, but for now we will concentrate on processing strings using pointers.

String processing using pointers usually involves at least three major steps.

1. Setting the pointer to the address of the beginning of the string.

2. Processing the string byte by byte, incrementing your pointer by one each time.

3. Always checking that the character that your pointer addresses is not the '\0' (end of string).

Let's see if we can incorporate these steps into counting the number of characters in a string (excluding the terminator).

```
static char name[25] = "count should be 18";
char *pntr;
int count = 0;

pntr = name;                        /* set pointer to start of string */

while ( *pntr != '\0' )             /* check for end of string */
{    count++;                       /* count character         */
     pntr++;                        /* point at next character */
}
```

Look at the code below. It works exactly as the code above. Why were we able to replace the loop condition "*pntr != '\0' ", with "*pntr"? Remember what causes loops to STOP and GO. '\0' is equivalent to 0, therefore, as soon as '*pntr' takes on the value '\0', the condition "*pntr" will be considered false, and the loop will stop.

```
static char name[25] = "count should be 18";
char *pntr;
int count = 0;

for ( pntr = name; *pntr; pntr++ )
     count++;
```

Once we are comfortable with string handling using pointers we can initialize strings as pointers instead of arrays. What we are about to do is declare a character pointer, then make it point to the first byte of the string constant we wish to use. Memory space is assigned to the string by the compiler.

```
char *message;
message = "message points to the 'm' in this string";
printf("%s\n", message);
```

It is often necessary to declare and initialize an array of strings instead of just one string. An array of strings can be represented as an array of character pointers. By looking at the rules of precedence and associativity, we can declare an array of character pointers as below.

```
char *many_strings[4];
```

In order to initialize an array of strings you provide an initializer list as you did with other array initialization, but this time each element in the initializer list will be a string literal inside double quotes.

```
char *q_and_a[] =
    { "Q. What is used to terminate a string in C?",
      "A. The null character.",
      "Q. How are strings usually represented in C?",
      "A. As character pointers or character arrays."
    };
```

STRINGS AND THE STANDARD LIBRARY

The Standard Library is a set of functions that accompanies every C compiler. These pre-written functions perform many of the most commonly needed tasks. Several of these deal with string processing. We will look at the basic string functions that find the length of a string, compare two strings, move a string, and append one string to another. Some other useful functions convert string type data to the different numeric data types. In ANSI compilers these functions are declared in "stdlib.h" and "string.h". Older compilers might be missing both these header files. If you have any trouble with your compiler, declare any function that doesn't return an integer at the top of your program or make your own "stdlib.h" and "string.h" with the necessary declarations. Some examples of these declarations are shown below.

```
char *strcpy();
long atol();
float atof();
```

The following 'str' type functions are declared in "string.h". The first one we will look at is `strlen()`, which is used to find the length of a string. You can send a character array name, a string pointer or a string literal, and `strlen()` returns an integer representing the length of the string.

```
int length;
length = strlen("this is a long string\n");
/* length is 22, '\n' counts as single character */
```

We can use `strcmp()` to compare two strings. Strings are compared one character at a time starting from the left of each string until the end of one of the strings is reached or a differing character is encountered. Upper-case and lower-case letters are considered different. Provide two string pointers (or literals, etc.). It returns an integer 0 if the two strings are exactly alike. It returns a negative number if the first string is "less than" the second string (i.e., first string is shorter than the second or its leftmost differing character has a lower ASCII code). It returns a positive number if the first string is "greater than" the second string (i.e., first string is longer than second or its leftmost differing character has a higher ASCII code).

What are 'x', 'y' and 'z' set to by the following code?

```
int   x, y, z;
char *s1, *s2, *s3, *s4;

s1 = "HELLO";
s2 = "hello";
s3 = "HELLO ";
s4 = "hello";

x = strcmp(s1, s2);
y = strcmp(s1, s3);
z = strcmp(s2, s4);
```

'x' is set to a negative value because 'H' and 'h' are different and 'H' has a lower ASCII code. Note that capitals are actually lower in the ASCII code than lower-case letters. If we switched the order of the strings, `strcmp(s2,s1)`, the result will be positive because 's2' is now our first string. 'y' is set to a negative value. Although the s1 and s3 are similar, s3 has an extra blank. 'z' is set to 0 because s2 and s4 are exactly alike. You can specify exactly how many characters you wish to compare by using `strncmp()`. You must provide a length after you list your two strings.

```
y = strncmp(s1, s3, 5);        /*   'y' is set to 0   */
```

To copy a string to a different area you can use `strcpy`. You must provide a string pointer or array name of the target area first, and a string pointer, string literal, or array name of the sending area second. This function returns a pointer to the first area (i.e., you can declare the function at the top of your program using `char *strcpy();`). This function doesn't check that the target area is large enough to hold the sending string. This means that you can accidentally alter other data if you aren't careful. To be safe, use `strncpy()`. Two examples are shown below.

```
strcpy(s2, "bye");
strncpy(s1, s3, 5);
```

To append one string to the end of another string, use `strcat()`. Provide two string pointers—first the target area, then the string to be appended. The null character that ends the first string will be replaced by the first character of the second string. The first area must be large enough to hold all characters of both strings, including a terminating '\0'. `strcat()` returns a pointer to the first area. Once again, if you want to be safe, you can use `strncat()`, which allows you to specify a maximum length to the append.

An example of `strcat()` and `strncat()` is shown below.

```
static char message[40] = "mary doesn't drink ";

strcat(message, "liquor");
strncat(message, ", just wine", 39);
```

There are several functions that will convert a string to a numeric data type. Each will receive a string pointer and return its own data type. With ANSI compilers, these functions will be declared in "stdlib.h", so that you should include this file at the top of your program. If you are using an older compiler declare each of these functions according to the data type it will return (i.e., ASCII to double is `atof()`, so declare it using `double atof();`).

```
#include <stdio.h>
#include <stdlib.h>

main()
{
    int x;
    double y;
    long z;

    static char number[] = "12345";

    x = atoi(number);      /* convert a string to an integer  */

    y = atof("75.125");    /* convert a string to a double    */

    z = atol(number);      /* convert a string to a long      */
    printf(" %d  %lf  %ld\n", x, y, z);
}
```

CHARACTER PROCESSING

Sometimes it is necessary to look at and process strings or keyboard input character by character. For instance, it might be necessary to know what type of character is being input, or to perform standard transformations on a character (e.g., converting a lower-case character to upper case). The macros in "ctype.h" provide us with several tools to make character processing easier (macros are used in much the same way as functions). Before any of these special character processing macros can be used, you must include "ctype.h" at the top of your program (use angle brackets because it is a system-supplied file).

```
#include <ctype.h>
```

The first set of macros we will look at are the 'is' macros. These macros check if a character belongs to a specific class of character. For instance, the `isdigit()` macro will check if the character is a decimal digit. The macros return non-zero if the character belongs to the class and 0 if it doesn't. A list of these 'is' macros and what they test for is shown below.

Macro	Test
`isalpha(c)`	is 'c' alphabetic.
`isalnum(c)`	is 'c' alphabetic or numeric.
`isupper(c)`	is 'c' an upper-case letter.
`islower(c)`	is 'c' a lower-case letter.
`isdigit(c)`	is 'c' a decimal digit (0 through 9).
`isxdigit(c)`	is 'c' a hexadecimal digit (0 through 9 or A through F, a through f).
`iscntrl(c)`	is 'c' a control character.
`isspace(c)`	is 'c' white space: ' ', '\n', '\t', '\f', '\r', or '\v'.
`isprint(c)`	is 'c' a printable character.
`ispunct(c)`	is 'c' a punctuation character.
`isascii(c)`	is 'c' a valid ASCII code.

An example of the use of these macros is shown below. (Assume that we included "ctype.h" at the top of the program.)

```
if ( isalpha(c) )
    printf("it's a letter\n");
else if ( isdigit(c) )
    printf("it's a digit\n");
else
    printf("it's not a letter or digit\n");
```

In addition to testing characters there are some common transformations that must be done on characters. The main transformations are

toascii(c)   –   return the ASCII value of 'c'. 'c' should be in the range of 0 through 127. toascii(c) will convert any values outside of this range into a value within the range (i.e., 158 might become 30).

toupper(c)   –   if 'c' is lower case, return upper case; otherwise return 'c'.

tolower(c)   –   if 'c' is upper case, return lower case; otherwise return 'c'.

These functions are commonly used when comparing strings. Remember that because of the way strcmp() works, strings like "ALBERT" and "Albert" are considered different. We can solve this problem by ensuring both strings have the same case before any comparison is done. A simple example of converting a string to upper case is shown below.

```
char *str = "a MixEd UP sTrINg";
char *p;

for ( p = str; *p; p++ )
    *p = toupper(*p);
```

PUTTING IT TOGETHER

TESTING STRINGS FOR SIMILARITY

Comparing two words for similarity is sometimes necessary because you may not know the exact spelling of the word you are searching for, or in the case of a database search, you may want to search for similar names (e.g., MacKenzie, McKenzie). We will develop the basics of this similarity tester in a separate file, "similar.c". It will receive two words, make copies of each word, then change both to lower case, strip any suffix, strip all vowels, then do a comparison of the two altered strings for equality. Our function will return 0 if the two words are similar and non-zero if they are not.

Our first task is to convert both strings to lower case. This will make any comparisons easier because we will have to do our comparisons in only one case. This is done in the function 'change_to_lower()'. The next step is to strip any suffix. We will set up a static array of string pointers representing the suffixes to check. (NOTE: Our list of suffixes is incomplete.) For each suffix, we would take the length, 'slen', and then check the last 'slen' bytes of our string to see if it matches the suffix. If it does match, we will put a '\0' at the beginning of the suffix in our original string (this effectively eliminates it). We will keep doing this until we have removed all suffixes from the end of the word.

The 'strip_vowels()' function is short but potentially confusing because it uses three pointers. We will create our new string from the old by using two pointers, 'leader' and 'trailer'. The 'leader' is used to inspect every character in the original string and is incremented for each character in the original string until '\0' is reached. The 'trailer' pointer is only incremented for every non-vowel. A character is assigned to '*trailer' only if it is not a vowel. This has the effect of creating a new string over the old one, which is missing the vowels. The statement '*trailer++ = *leader;' will assign the character pointed to by 'leader' to the character pointed to by 'trailer', then increment the 'trailer' pointer.

To find vowels, we will compare each character against an array of vowels. The terminating condition for our search is either a match being found, or the end of the vowel string being encountered. We know a match has occurred if the pointer doesn't point to '\0' (end of string). Please note that there is a function, strpbrk(), which acts in a similar manner.

Several of our functions were declared as returning pointers to characters (strings). This is done by placing a '*' before the function name indicating the function returns a pointer, and using char to indicate the pointer type. These functions were set up in this manner just in case they were to be used in expressions or as arguments. An example of the use of one of these functions in a statement is shown below.

```
printf("%s\n", strip_vowels( s1 ));
```

```
/* SIMILAR.C  This file contains functions necessary to compare two
              words for similarity. The technique used is to convert
              copies of the two words being compared into lower case,
              then strip any suffixes, strip any vowels, and finally
              compare the two altered strings. This work is done in
              'similar()' which returns 0 if the two strings are
              similar, and non-zero if they are not.
*/
#include <string.h>
#include <ctype.h>

#define NULL 0
#define TRUE 1
#define FALSE 0
#define MAX_WORD 25

char *strip_vowels( char *s );
char *strip_suffix( char *s );
char *change_to_lower( char *s );

int similar(char *first, char *second)
{
    char fcopy[MAX_WORD + 1], scopy[MAX_WORD + 1];
    fcopy[MAXWORD] = '\0';
    scopy[MAXWORD] = '\0';
    strncpy(fcopy, first, MAX_WORD);
    strncpy(scopy, second, MAX_WORD);
    change_to_lower(fcopy);
```

```
        change_to_lower(scopy);

        strip_suffix(fcopy);
        strip_suffix(scopy);
        strip_vowels(fcopy);
        strip_vowels(scopy);

        return ( strncmp(fcopy, scopy, MAX_WORD) );
}

char  *change_to_lower( char *string )
{   char *p;
    for ( p = string; *p; p++ )
        *p = tolower( *p );
    return ( string );
}

char *strip_suffix( char *s )
{
    int i, len, slen, suffix_found;
    char *p;
    static char *suffixes[] = { "al", "ate", "ed", "ence",
                                "ent", "est", "ing",
                                "ion", "ly", NULL };
    len = strlen(s);

    do {
        suffix_found = FALSE;

        for ( i = 0; suffixes[i] != NULL; i++ )
        {
          slen = strlen(suffixes[i]);

          if ( len >= slen )
          {
            p = s + len - slen  ;

            if ( strcmp ( p, suffixes[i] ) == 0)
            {
                *p = '\0';
                suffix_found = TRUE;
                len = p - s;
                break;
            }
          }
        }
      } while ( len > 0 && suffix_found);

    return( s ) ;
}

char *strip_vowels( char *s )
{
    static char *vowels = "aeiouAEIOU";
    char *leader, *trailer, *vow_ptr;
```

```
for ( leader = s, trailer = s; *leader; leader++ )
{
    for( vow_ptr = vowels;
         *vow_ptr && ( *vow_ptr != *leader );
         vow_ptr++)
         ;                                          /* NULL BODY  */

    if ( *vow_ptr == '\0' )                         /* not a vowel  */
        *trailer++ = *leader;
}
*trailer = '\0';                    /* terminate string with NULL */
return ( s );
}
```

LABORATORY 6

1. Write a program that will determine if a string entered by a user is null. Print a message. For a refinement, convert the program into a function 'strnull', which receives a string pointer and returns the integer 1, if it is null, and the integer 0, if it isn't null.

2. Write a program that will replace any single character in a string with another character. Test your program by changing the w's in the following string to r's.

    "be vewy vewy quiet, this is wabbit countwy"

    For a refinement, convert this into a function 'chngechar()', which receives a string pointer, the character to replace, and the character to replace it with.

3. A mail-order software house has both American and Canadian customers. Canadian postal codes follow a special pattern; letter, digit, letter, space, digit, letter, digit. Write the code to validate these seven-character codes.

4. Write an integer function called 'getnum()' that uses 'getchar()' to get a numeric string, then converts it to an integer and returns it to the calling function.

5. Write a function 'month_name' that receives an integer representing month number, and returns the name of the month, in the form of a string pointer. You must use an array of string pointers inside your function, as shown below.

    ```
    static char *month[] = { "illegal month", "January",
                             "February", "March",
                             etc. etc.
                           };
    ```

6. Enhance the similarity tester described in this chapter by including functions to strip prefixes from a word and to replace double occurrences of a consonant with a single occurrence. Also consider a more efficient way to search for suffixes. (HINT: Compare the ending to ordered lists of suffixes of different lengths.)

7
FILES

Learning how to use files is very important since they enable the external storage of information. We will look at the use of named files in C. Files are little more than a sequence of bytes stored on an external device like a disk. This means that a file is really just a special string stored on an external device. In this chapter we will concentrate on using disk files.

With named files we need to be able to:

- Open the file to read or write data.
- Read data from the file.
- Write data to the file.
- Close the file.

Before we use any file we must always include a list of definitions important to file use, which is contained in "stdio.h". At the top of our program we will put

```
#include <stdio.h>
```

We must also declare variables for any file we open so that we can refer to files by variable names (e.g., 'infile') instead of external system names (e.g., "inventory.dat"). All internal file names must be declared as pointers to a FILE. Declaring your files as simple FILE's instead of pointers to FILE's is a common programming error.

```
FILE   *infile, *outfile;
```

OPENING AND CLOSING FILES

To open a file, we use the fopen() function. This returns a pointer to a file. We must provide the function with a string representing the external name of the file, and a string representing how we wish to use the file (will we be reading or writing?). The file name can be a string literal or the variable name of a string. The function will return a valid file pointer if no errors have occurred and NULL if there is an error. An example of opening "new.dat" to write is found below.

```
outfile = fopen( "new.dat", "w" );
```

The more common open modes are "w" for write, "r" for read and "a" for append (with append, a new file will be created if no file existed; otherwise, new data is appended to the end of an existing file).

When we open a file, we should check for the possibility of an error. For instance, we could try to open a file to read and find that it doesn't exist. Remember that the fopen() returns NULL if the open was not successful. If we get a NULL returned we could print an error message and quit the program.

The exit() function allows us to quit the program anywhere within the program. This is a very dangerous function if used indiscriminately because your program will have more than one possible exit point (potentially causing debugging problems). The inability to open a file is a critical run time error and justifies the use of this function. The exit() function can be used to return a value that can be used by the operating system. By convention, returning 1 indicates some type of error.

To close a file, we just use the fclose() and provide a file pointer name. You should close your files as soon as you have finished using them (even if this is near the beginning of the program.)

```
#include <stdio.h>
int main()
{
    FILE *infile, *outfile;
    int c;
    static char *filename = "myfile.dat";

    if ( (infile = fopen(filename, "r")) == NULL )
    { printf("\ncannot open %s", filename);
      exit(1)
    }
                                    /* file processing logic goes here */
    .
    .
    .
    fclose( infile );
}
```

READING AND WRITING DATA

To use files we must be able to get characters or groups of characters and write characters or groups of characters. When we read files we must also be able to detect when we have reached the end of the file. There is a whole set of functions in the standard library (present with every C compiler) that allows us to do this.

The function that gets a single character is getc(). It has the format

```
int getc( filepointer );
```

The getc() function gets a single character from the file specified by the file pointer (this file must already be open for reading). It will return either the character read from the file or a special EOF value if the end of the input file has been reached. It returns an integer because the EOF (end of file) cannot be represented in a single byte on all machines. To read many characters from a file, we can put the getc() function in a loop. The following code reads an entire file (which was previously opened) and displays it on the screen using putchar(). EOF is defined in "stdio.h" and we must enclose "c = getc(textfile)" in parentheses because of precedence. We want to read first, then check 'c' against EOF.

```
while ( (c = getc(textfile)) != EOF )
    putchar(c);
```

The putc() function writes a single character to a file specified by the file pointer. You must specify the character to be written (as either a literal or integer or character variable) and the file you wish to write to. The following code copies one file to another. Both files have been opened previously.

```
while ( (c = getc(oldfile)) != EOF )
    putc(c, newfile);
```

Reading and writing groups of characters, like lines of a text file or records in a data file, is a very important part of file processing. The standard library provides several functions that allow us to do this more easily.

We have already looked at some very useful input/output functions in earlier chapters, such as printf(), scanf(), gets(), and puts(). These functions are so useful that functions very similar to these exist in the standard library and work with files instead of the screen or keyboard.

We will first look at formatted input/output for files using fprintf() and fscanf(). These work exactly like printf() and scanf(), except that you must provide a file pointer name before the format string in both cases. Of course, the file must be opened in such a manner that reading is allowed when the fscanf() is used and to allow writing when the fprintf() is used. Furthermore you should always check for end of file every time that fscanf() is used. fscanf() returns the number of successful conversions made or EOF if end of file has been reached.

In the code below, we will read through a file with an account number (long), a debit/credit code (1 for credit, 0 for debit), and an amount (double). We will keep a running tally of credits and debits. We will keep reading until EOF has been reached or an error record has been encountered (fewer than three conversions).

```
#include <stdio.h>
main()
{
    long acct_no;
    double debits = 0, credits = 0, amount = 0;
    int code, converts, error = 0;
    FILE *infile;
```

```
   if ( (infile = fopen("trans.dat","r")) == NULL )
   { printf("could not open 'trans.dat'");
     exit(1);
   };

   converts = fscanf(infile, "%ld%d%lf",
                     &acct_no, &code, &amount);

   while ( converts == 3 )
   {
      if ( code == 0 )
         debits += amount;
      else if ( code == 1 )
         credits += amount;

      converts = fscanf(infile, "%ld%d%lf",
                  &acct_no, &code, &amount);
   }

   if ( converts == EOF )
      printf("total debits %lf  total credits %lf",
              debits, credits);
   else
      printf("error in file, processing terminated");
   fclose(infile);
}
```

Some other useful functions are fgets() and fputs(). To use fgets() just provide the name of a character array or character pointer, the size of the character array (include one character for the null terminator), and the name of the file pointer you wish to use. fgets() will continue getting characters until one of the following conditions has been met:

1. A new line, '\n', has been encountered.

2. It has read n - 1 characters (one character less than the size of the character array).

3. It has encountered EOF.

fgets() returns a pointer to the string it has just read in. If an error has occurred or end of file has occurred, then fgets() will return NULL. To determine what actually caused the NULL being returned, you can use feof(). feof() requires that you send it a valid filepointer. It returns a non- zero integer if it has encountered EOF and 0 if it has not.

```
#include <stdio.h>
#define LINE_LENGTH   81
main()
{
   FILE *infile;
   char datain[LINE_LENGTH];
   int out_of_data = 0;
```

```
infile = fopen("test.dat", "r");
                        /* get a line of data up to 80 characters
                           long from 'infile'. Deposit this line
                           in 'datain'. If a NULL is returned
                           check if it is really  end-of-file using
                           'feof()'.                              */

while( !out_of_data )
{
    if ( fgets(datain, LINE_LENGTH, in_file) == NULL )
    {
        if ( feof( infile ) )
            out_of_data = 1;
    } else
/* process data here */
    .
    .
    .
}
```

fputs() writes a string (minus its null terminator, '\0') to a specified file. It returns an integer, with non-zero signifying a successful write, and 0 signifying some type of error. The return value is not commonly used. Unlike the puts() used in earlier chapters, fputs() does not append a newline ('\n') to the string when it outputs the string. Provide fputs() with the string first and the file pointer second. An example is shown below:

```
fputs("how are you\n", outfile);
```

FILES AND COMMAND LINE ARGUMENTS

One good use for C is to write small file-processing programs called utilities, which operate on a variety of files. To make utilities useful we must be able to get information from the user's command line. Look at the command line below:

```
copy file1 file2
```

The command line consists of three words or arguments, "copy", "file1", and "file2". "copy" is the name of the program that executes the desired task, and the second and third arguments (words) are the file names we wish to use. In order to make our programs interact with this command line, we need to access the words on the command line.

We will write a program called "copy.c", which will copy one file to another, getting the filenames from the command line. We can write any program so that the main() in the program receives the number of words in the command line and a pointer to the first word on that line.

```
#include <stdio.h>
int main( int wordcount, char *words[] )
{
    FILE *fopen(), *infile, *outfile;
    int c;
```

```
    if ( wordcount != 3 )
    { printf("\ncopy command requires two filenames");
      exit(1);
    }

    if( (infile = fopen(words[1], "r")) == NULL )
    { printf("\ncannot open %s", words[1]);
      exit(1);
    }

    if( (outfile = fopen(words[2], "w")) == NULL )
    { printf("\ncannot open %s", words[2]);
      exit(1);
    }

    while ( (c = getc(infile)) != EOF )
        putc(c, outfile);

    fclose(infile);
    fclose(outfile);
}
```

The code above demonstrates the following points.

1. The main() always receives the number of words on the command line as an integer first, and the words themselves as an array of string pointers second. The main() is similar to any other function except that it returns a value using exit() instead of return.

2. Both 'infile' and 'outfile' are defined as pointers to a FILE.

3. If there were three words on the command line, we could access those words via 'words[0]', 'words[1]', and 'words[2]'.

4. Since this program requires two filenames to work properly, we could check for this through the 'wordcount'. It must be three, since the program name is also included in the 'wordcount'.

5. Once we have received the string pointers, we can use them for our file names in our fopen() statements.

6. When we open both files, we test for an error and exit from the program if one occurs. We will return the value 1 to the operating system because that indicates that the program terminated abnormally.

7. We closed both files before exiting our program.

ADVANCED FILE HANDLING

Binary Files

Up to this point we have been dealing with text files. These are simple to handle because an assumption is made that bytes in the file will represent characters (ASCII codes between 0 and 127). If we ever encounter a -1, (EOF) we will interpret it as an end-of-file indicator.

There are two features of text file handling that could cause problems with more advanced file handling. First, on some systems, characters are automatically added to a file on writing, or stripped in reading the file. This is called translation. For example, on some systems, writing a '\n', will actually cause a two-character combination, '\r' and '\n', to be written out. This could cause problems if we tried to directly access individual locations within the file and this translation process is occurring. We wouldn't know where we are in the file because we would have to know all the characters that caused a translation.

The second problem involves the use of the EOF as an indication of the end of file. This really will work only if we can expect all data and all stored bytes to be character type data. If this is not true, such as when we try to store program data as it is stored in memory, a program processing until EOF might end prematurely. This is because some of the data within the file could accidentally trip the EOF indicator.

The answer to both problems is to use the binary file, which doesn't perform any character translation, and to change the way we treat the end of file. In order to open a binary file, use "rb" or "wb", instead of "r" or "w" when providing the open mode for `fopen()`. Instead of checking for EOF we will use the `feof()` function mentioned in the previous sections.

Two functions that are often used with binary files are `fwrite()` and `fread()`. `fwrite()` will write a given number of data items from any memory location to a specified file pointer. You must provide `fwrite()` with the address of the array or memory variable, the size of the data item, the number of data items, and the file pointer (in that order). An example is shown below.

```
FILE   *binary_file;
static float array[] = { 1.0, 2.0, 3.0, 4.0 };
int q = 6000;

binary_file = fopen("test.dat", "wb");
fwrite(&q, sizeof(int), 1, binary_file);
fwrite(array, sizeof(float),
        sizeof(array)/sizeof(float), binary_file);
```

`fread()` will read a given number of data items into an array or memory variable from a file. You must provide the same parameters in the same order as in `fwrite()`. It will return the number of data items that were successfully read. If it doesn't return the expected number, you can check for end of file by using the `feof()` function.

Direct File Addressing

One of the advantages of UNIX/C concept of files is that you are able to directly address any byte in a file. This ability to jump about in a file allows us to create databases, indexed files, and relative files. What we need is a function to tell us where we are relative to the beginning of the file (the `ftell()`), and a function to let us seek a particular position within a file (the `fseek()`).

The `ftell()` receives a file pointer (filename) and returns a long integer representing the position of the next byte to be read or written. A long integer is returned because files can be very large (millions of bytes) and an integer range on some machines is small (e.g., 65536). The example below reads through a file, detecting every end of record (any '\n'), and stores the file position of the beginning of each record in an array 'recptrs'. We use `ftell()` to determine file position.

```
#define  TOT_RECPTRS 250

long int recptrs[TOT_RECPTRS];
int byte, count = 0;

recptrs[0] = 1L;
while ( (byte = getc(infile)) != EOF )
{
  if ( byte == '\n' )
    if( ++count < TOT_RECPTRS )
        recptrs[count] = ftell(infile);
}
```

The fseek() receives a file pointer (filename), a long integer representing a distance to move, and an integer representing the mode. The mode is where we move from, or our reference point, 0 is for the beginning of file, 1 is for our current position, and 2 is for the end of file. These different reference points allow us to process a file backwards from the end of file to the beginning of file. Be careful to provide a long integer for the distance to move (also called the offset). A few examples of fseek statements are shown below.

```
fseek(tempfile, 150L, 0);
fseek(infile, recptrs[23], 0);
fseek(tempfile, -20L, 2);
```

LABORATORY 7

1. Write a program that will append one text file to the end of another text file. Let the user provide the two filenames. Call the program 'append.c'.

2. Some programming editors use tabs instead of multiple spaces for indenting. This can cause problems if the program is later loaded into a wordprocessor. Write a program to 'detab' a text file. You should replace every occurrence of a tab, '\t', with six spaces. Use command line arguments for the filename. For an enhancement, get the number of replacement spaces from the command line also.

3. Write a program, "paste.c", which takes any two files, and pastes each record of the second file onto the end of the corresponding record of the first file. For example:

File 1	File 2
aaaa\n	qqq\n
bbb\n	rr\n
ccc\n	sssss\n

Pasted File (File 3)
aaaaqqq\n
bbbrr\n
cccsssss\n

Write your program using command line arguments.

4. Load an array of floats with numbers 0.0 through 99.0. Save this array, as it would appear in memory, to a file. Now write a program that will load and display any five-element subarray of the 100-element array. (i.e., five-element array starting at the seventh element, the fortieth, etc.). You are not allowed to load the whole array (100 elements) at once.

8
WORKING WITH BITS

Two important advantages of C are that with pointers we can easily get to any byte in memory, and with bit operators we can alter or inspect individual bits in any byte. These two capabilities give us considerable control over the 'machine' and mean that C can be used instead of assembler in many instances.

Before we go on, a warning is in order. Although C is often called a portable assembler because of its bitwise operators, the use of these operators tends to make programs less portable. This is because the effect of some bitwise operators is dependent on the features of the machine that the program runs on. It is wise to use these operators only when there is no other choice.

Now let's get to the 'bit-banging'. The subjects we will concentrate on are: setting and clearing individual bits, determining the status of an individual bit, and forming masks.

In reality, it is not possible to access an individual bit in any byte in C or any other language. Only bytes or words can be accessed. What we can do is to set up special patterns so that, when the pattern is applied to the byte or word, parts of the byte will be changed and parts will be left unchanged depending on the programmer's wishes. These special patterns are called masks. We will learn how to set up masks for use with the major bit operators.

ORING

We can use the '|' operator to set individual bits within a byte or integer. We can set a bit in a particular byte or integer by setting up a special bit pattern called a mask, and oring this bit pattern with our original value.

Once we have decided which bits we want set (i.e., set to 1), and which bits we want left unchanged, we can set up our mask (bit pattern). We set up our mask by placing a '1' in any spot where we want to set the original to '1', and a '0' where we want the original to remain unchanged.

70

Let's look at oring with `char` type data (usually eight bits). ALL EXAM-PLES SHOWN HERE ARE MACHINE DEPENDENT. Let's start with our original, which we will call 'byte'. The bit pattern for 'byte' is shown below:

```
0    0    0    1    1    1    0    0
```

The value for this bit pattern is found by multiplying each 1 by its digit value, and adding up the results.

128's	64's	32's	16's	8's	4's	2's	1's
↓	↓	↓	↓	↓	↓	↓	↓
0	0	0	1	1	1	0	0

The value for our bit pattern above is 28 decimal (1 * 16 + 1 * 8 + 1 * 4). When you are working with bit patterns it is actually more natural to work with hexadecimal numbers rather than decimal. There is no easy correspondence between the digits of a decimal number and the bit pattern itself. With hexadecimal numbers, every hexadecimal digit corresponds to exactly four bits of the bit pattern. The hexadecimal value for the bit pattern above is 0x1C. The 1 corresponds to the leftmost four bits (0 0 0 1), and the C corresponds to the rightmost four bits (1 1 0 0). Of course, larger values such as `int`s will require more hexadecimal digits to represent them. A list of the hexadecimal digits and their decimal and bit pattern equivalents is shown below.

Hex	Dec	Bit Pattern
0	0	0 0 0 0
1	1	0 0 0 1
2	2	0 0 1 0
3	3	0 0 1 1
4	4	0 1 0 0
5	5	0 1 0 1
6	6	0 1 1 0
7	7	0 1 1 1
8	8	1 0 0 0
9	9	1 0 0 1
A	10	1 0 1 0
B	11	1 0 1 1
C	12	1 1 0 0
D	13	1 1 0 1
E	14	1 1 1 0
F	15	1 1 1 1

Using our original bit pattern, we might wish to set the eighth bit from the right without changing any others. We must put a '1' in our mask whenever we wish to set the bit, and a '0' when we don't. If we wish only to set the eighth bit from the right, our bit pattern will be all 0's except for a '1' in the eighth bit from the right. Our bit pattern would look like this:

```
1    0    0    0    0    0    0    0
```

This bit pattern has a numeric value as well. If we were to multiply each digit by its digit value and add the results, we would get 128 or 0x80. An example of using these bit patterns is shown below. Note how we are assigning a numeric value to 'byte', a character. `unsigned char` type data can be treated as integers with a very small range (0 through 255).

```
unsigned char byte;
unsigned int mask, test ;

byte  = 0x1C;
mask  = 0x80;
test  = byte | mask;          /* our test is set to 156 or 0x9C */
```

Our original number had a value of 0x1C (decimal 28), because the middle three bits were on (set to '1'). Now we made the eighth bit from the right a '1' by using our mask. The resultant bit pattern is shown below and its value is decimal 156 (1 * 128 + 1 * 16 + 1 * 8 + 1 * 4) or 0x9C (bit pattern 1 0 0 1, which is 9, and bit pattern 1 1 0 0, which is C or 12).

    1 0 0 1 1 1 0 0

ANDING—TESTING AND CLEARING BITS

The and operator, '&', is used to clear bits (i.e., set bits to 0). The '&' works so that, if there is a zero value in the corresponding positions of either the mask or the original, the result in that position will be a zero. It is commonly used to test the values of individual bits and to reset bits to 0. We must use a mask, just as we did with the 'I' operator, but this time we put a '0' in our mask for every position we want cleared and a '1' for every position we want unchanged.

Let's use the '&' operator to test an individual bit, then to clear a bit. We will test the leftmost bit of a character. If it is set, we will turn it off (set it to 0), otherwise we will leave it unchanged. To test the leftmost bit, we will set up a mask with a '1' in the leftmost position and 0's for all other positions. This means that the seven rightmost bits of our result are automatically set to 0. The leftmost bit remains unchanged. If it was originally '1' the value for our result would be 128 (the digit value of the leftmost bit); otherwise, it would be 0.

Now, if that leftmost bit is set, we will clear it. This means setting up a mask that will clear only the leftmost bit and leave all other bits unchanged (a '0' in the leftmost bit, with all other bits being '1'). The mask value is 127 (or hexadecimal 7F). The code is found below:

```
#define TEST_MASK 0x80
                        /* decimal 128  or  1 0 0 0 0 0 0 0  */
#define CLEAR_MASK 0x7F
                        /* decimal 127  or  0 1 1 1 1 1 1 1  */
char  c;

if ( ( c & TEST_MASK ) != 0 )
    c &= CLEAR_MASK;                        /* acts the same as:
                                        c = c & clearing_mask; */
```

OTHER BIT OPERATORS

Shifting

You can shift the complete bit pattern in a character or integer by a positive number of bits using the shift operators, '>>' and '<<'. It will probably come as no surprise that '>>' is a right shift, and '<<' is a left shift.

The operations are machine dependent. This means that programs using these operators are not always portable. On left shifts, the bits left open on the right are always filled with zeros, but on right shifts of signed integers the positions left open on the left are sometimes filled with 0 and sometimes filled with the original value of the leftmost bit (which could have been either '1' or '0'). Right shifts of unsigned integer type variables are always padded on the left with zeros. Some examples of shift operations are shown below.

```
unsigned char x, y, original ;

original =  0x3C;         /* bit pattern   0 0 1 1 1 1 0 0  */
x = original >> 2;        /* x is 0x0F or  0 0 0 0 1 1 1 1  */
y = original << 5;        /* y is 0x80 or  1 0 0 0 0 0 0 0  */
```

One's Complement

The complement operator '~', takes any character or integer and reverses the value of every bit in the bit pattern. All 1's in the bit pattern will be changed to 0's and all 0's to 1's.

```
char x, original;

original =  0x3C;         /* bit pattern  0 0 1 1 1 1 0 0   */
x =~  original;          /* x is 0xC3  or  1 1 0 0 0 0 1 1  */
```

Exclusive or

The exclusive or operator, '^', takes an original and a mask, and if the corresponding bits in both are the same, will set the resultant bits to 0, and if they are different, will set them to 1.

```
unsigned char  x, mask, original;

mask = 0xF0;             /* bit pattern  1 1 1 1 0 0 0 0   */
original = 0x3C;         /* bit pattern  0 0 1 1 1 1 0 0   */
x = original ^ mask;     /* x is 0xCC or 1 1 0 0 1 1 0 0   */
```

PUTTING IT TOGETHER

SETTING PARITY

The transmission of data between computers and devices is prone to different types of error. One possible error is that when transmitting a 'byte', one of the bits is changed or flipped. One technique that was developed to catch this type of error was parity-checking. The technique is simple; use only seven bits of an eight-bit byte for the data, and leave the eighth bit as a parity bit. We will count the number of bits that are set in the data bits, then either set the parity bit or leave it alone, in order to get the total number of bits set to an even number. In other words, our eight-bit bytes should always have an even number of bits set. This is called even parity (we could have also chosen odd-parity).

Now, how will we do it? Our first task will be to test all the data bits and just count the number that are set. After this is done, if the count is odd, we need to make it even so we will set the parity bit. We could test the data bits by setting up seven different masks, anding them with the byte, and tallying for each one set. A much easier way would be to set up one mask to test the rightmost bit and shift each bit in the byte into the test location, one at a time. We will set up a function called 'parity_count()' which will receive a character, and count the number of bits set in the first seven bits. Our function 'even_parity()' will receive a character and set it for even parity. It will use our 'parity_count()' function.

```c
/*   parity.c           This program will set even parity for
                        characters between 'a' (ascii 97) and
                        and 'l' (ascii 109). It uses
                        'parity_count' to count the '1' bits in
                        the rightmost 7 bits and 'even_parity()'
                        to set the parity bit if the count is odd.
*/

#define SET_HIGH_BIT 0x80
#define TEST_LOW_BIT 0x01
#define TEST_HIGH_BIT 0x80

int parity( unsigned char byte );
unsigned char even_parity( unsigned char byte );

main()
{
   unsigned char c;
   for ( c = 'a';  c < 'l'; c++ )
     printf(" char %c, ascii %d, parity count %d, parity bit %d\n",
            c,
            c,
            parity_count(c),
            ( even_parity(c) & TEST_HIGH_BIT ) ? 1 : 0 );
}

int parity_count( unsigned char byte )
{
   int count = 0;
   int bit;

   for ( bit = 0; bit < 7; bit++ )
      count += byte >> bit & TEST_LOW_BIT;

   return ( count );

}

unsigned char even_parity( unsigned char byte )
{
   if ( parity_count(byte) % 2 )
      byte |= SET_HIGH_BIT;

   return ( byte );
}
```

LABORATORY 8

1. We want to do some bit manipulation with a two-byte integer. Set up masks to do the following:

   a. clear the tenth bit from the right.

   b. set the sixth and ninth bit from the right.

2. Write the C code that will test if a character is not a true ASCII character. The leftmost bit of an ASCII character must be 0.

3. Write the C code to determine the numeric value of the leftmost three bits of a character (the value should be between 0 and 7).

4. Write a function that will flip the rightmost four bits of a byte with the leftmost four bits of a byte (this is an important function for dealing with packed decimal numbers).

9

DYNAMIC MEMORY ALLOCATION

We have already used arrays to store groups of similar-sized elements. There is one major handicap to the use of arrays—the size of the array is fixed when the program is compiled. Many data sets can vary widely in size, so that one time it might consist of 40 elements and the next time it might be 400. With arrays, we can compensate for this by defining our array to contain 400 elements, but this would be very wasteful.

The solution to this problem is to reserve memory as you need it, during the program run. This is called dynamic memory allocation. It is commonly used for any data sets that may vary greatly in size. It is also commonly used for linked lists. C has several functions that help us reserve and free up memory during a program run.

The entire concept of dynamically allocating storage revolves around two requirements.

Needs

1. We need a function or functions that will find out where there is free memory available for us. Ideally it will give us the address of that memory area.

2. We might need a function that releases some of our data areas when we no longer need them. If we keep reserving memory and never release it, we'll eventually run out of memory (it will become clogged with our garbage).

The standard library has two functions, `calloc()` and `malloc()`, which will find free memory available for us and return a pointer to the beginning of this area. These functions are declared in 'stdlib.h' in ANSI compilers but might have to be declared individually in older compilers. To be consistent these functions always return the same type of pointer, regardless of the eventual use of the memory area. Since a generic (all-purpose) pointer is returned, it is left up to the programmer to cast that pointer into the correct type. In ANSI C, these functions return a pointer to a `void` (`void *`). In older compilers these functions return a pointer to a `char`.

'calloc()'

This is a function that makes it easy to reserve areas to hold arrays.

We send it the number of elements we want to reserve, and the size of an individual element.

It will return a pointer to the address where that memory is available, or the NULL pointer if it isn't available.

`calloc()` initializes all elements to zero.

Since `calloc()` only returns `void` pointers (ANSI) or `char` pointers (Old C), we must cast the pointer into the pointer type we wish.

Let's see how we would reserve an area for 25 integers using `calloc()`. We would send it 25 for the number of elements, `sizeof(int)` for the size of the element, and we would get back a pointer to a `void` or character, not an integer. We could cast the pointer to an integer pointer using `(int *)`.

```
#include <stdlib.h>

int *int_ptr;
int_ptr = (int *) calloc(25, sizeof(int));
```

It was wise for us to use the `sizeof(int)` instead of literals such as '2' or '4', since `sizeof(int)` will work on any machine; '2' would only work on machines with two-byte integers.

We now have 'int_ptr' pointing to the beginning of an area large enough to hold 25 integers, and we could set up an array in that area or just use a pointer to process that area. Here we will load the area with all even numbers between 2 and 50.

```
ptr = int_ptr;
for ( i = 2; i <= 50; i += 2 )
   *ptr++ =  i;
```

'malloc()'

This is a 'no frills' version of the `calloc()`. It does not initialize the elements to 0.

You must send it the total number of bytes you wish to reserve.

It returns a pointer to an area of free memory large enough to hold your data. A NULL pointer will be returned if insufficient space is available. Like `calloc()`, it returns a pointer to a `void` (ANSI) or to a character (Old C) so that you must cast it to the correct pointer type.

```
long int *pointer1;
pointer1 = (long int *) malloc(sizeof(long int));
```

In the example above, 'pointer1' is set to point to an area which has been reserved for one long integer. Since `malloc` returns a pointer to a `void` or character, we must cast this result into a pointer to a long integer (the data type of 'pointer1').

'free()'

This function releases memory that was previously allocated by either a
calloc() or a malloc().

You must send it the beginning address of a data area previously allocated
by calloc() or malloc().

```
free(big_ptr);
```

The code below combines file handling and dynamic memory allocation.
It loads up to 1250 integers into memory, allocating storage only 25 integers
at a time.

- "int *int_ptrs[BLOCKS]" declares an array of pointers to integers. We
  will save the starting positions of each of our allocated areas in this
  array.

- We will use fscanf() to get our integers. It will return an EOF when
  it hits the end of file.

- Every time we hit an even multiple of 25 (i.e., 0, 25, 50, etc.) we must
  allocate new storage. We can check for this using the modulus operator, '%'.

```
#include <stdio.h>
#include <stdlib.h>
#define BLOCK_SIZE 25
#define BLOCKS 50
#define MAX_CNT (BLOCKS * BLOCK_SIZE)

FILE *infile;
int *int_ptrs[BLOCKS], *ptr;
int count = 0, i = 0, value, innum;

infile = fopen("test.dat", "r");
while ( (value = fscanf(infile, "%d", &innum)) != EOF
                && (count < MAX_CNT) )
{
    if ( count % BLOCK_SIZE == 0 )
    {
        int_ptrs[i] = (int *) calloc(BLOCK_SIZE, sizeof(int));
        ptr = int_ptrs[i];
        i++;
    }
    *ptr++ = innum;
    count++;
}
```

LABORATORY 9

1. Write the `calloc()` statements necessary to reserve memory for the following:

   a. 100 floating point numbers.

   b. 25 pointers to floating point numbers.

2. Use `malloc()` to write a program that will read 256 byte blocks of text into memory from a file "messages" until an end of file is detected or ten records have been read.

3. Write a program that will read in up to 15 strings from a user at the keyboard. Use `malloc()` and `strlen()` to reserve memory for each string as they are entered. Display all strings after they have been entered.

4. Write a function 'talloc' that temporarily allocates memory. It will return a pointer to a memory area just like `malloc()` and `calloc()` but it will automatically free any area allocated by the function after ten new allocations. Use a static array of `char` pointers to store the addresses of the allocated memory.

10

STRUCTURES

We have already looked at grouping elements together using arrays. The special requirement to use an array was that all elements be of the same type, and each element be identified by a number. We can use a structure to group dissimilar elements and identify each element by a name. This allows us to group several elements into a higher-level data item, which sometimes results in a more logical treatment of higher level problems. Through the use of structures we are allowed to create data types that more closely model the objects of the actual problem.

We might want a high-level data item or structure to describe a car. For our purposes, a car can be adequately described using a string for the name, a float for engine size, an integer for the number of cylinders, and a float for the acceleration. This is how we would set up our structure.

```
                              ── Name structure type
    struct car      {   char *name;
                        float liters;                }  Define
                        int cylinders;                  members
                        float acceleration;
    Keyword         };
    'struct'
```

We have defined only a template or pattern for the data type 'car'. Now that we have the template set up, we can declare variables of type 'car' as below. Let's declare a structure 'sportscar' which follows the same pattern as 'car'.

```
    struct car sportscar;
```

We can actually define the template, declare actual occurrences (or variables) and initialize all the elements in one step. An example is shown below:

```
                      ┌────── Name structure type
struct car      {   char *name;
                    float liters;
                    int cylinders;     } Define
                    float acceleration;   members
Keyword
'struct'
                } sportscar = { "911 TURBO",
                                  2.6,
Declare a                         5,            } Initialize
variable of                       5.1             with data
type 'car'                      };
```

We can use the whole structure or individual elements in the structure. We can access the elements of a structure by listing the structure (occurrence) name, followed by a '.', followed by the member. If we wanted to access 'cylinders' in 'sportscar' to change the value to a six, we would use the following statement.

```
sportscar.cylinders = 6;
```

Let's declare a new type of car called 'family_car' and access a few members.

```
struct car family_car;

family_car.name = "buick";
family_car.cylinders = 8;
printf("%s has %d cylinders\n", family_car.name,
                        family_car.cylinders);
```

We can perform any operations on the individual members that are allowed for the member data type. Please note that we can access the members of 'family_car' (and previously 'sportscar') but not 'car' itself. 'car' is only a conceptual pattern to describe all cars; 'family_car' and 'sportscar' are actual occurrences of this pattern.

USING STRUCTURES

Structures are a constructed data type, a data type that we have created ourselves. Although all operations that are legal for a member's data type are legal for the structure member, there are some restrictions on operations using an entire structure. The only operations that are allowed by the ANSI Standard on complete structures are the assignment of structures to other structures of the same type (using '='), passing complete structures to functions as arguments, and having a function return a complete structure. Some older compilers will not allow any of the these capabilities. Arithmetic and string operations are permitted only on structure members, not on the structure as a whole.

Once we have defined our structure, we can use it like other data types. We can create arrays of structures; we could use structures as members of other structures, establish pointers to structures, and pass or return structures to or from functions (ANSI compilers). Let's look at each of these in turn.

To demonstrate the use of structures, we will first set up a structure definition to describe a diamond and then use it in a variety of ways. The main features that describe a diamond are color, size, and clarity. Color can be represented as an integer since there are about ten color groups. Clarity can also be represented as an integer since there are only eight clarity classifications. Size is a `float` (carats). We will also need a number to identify the diamond. We will use a `long` for the 'id_no'. We will first define our structure as below, then use it in several examples.

```
struct diamond {
            long id_no;
            int color;
            int clarity;
            float carats;
        };
```

It is common practice to place structure definitions like these in separate header files, along with important symbol definitions, because very often these structure definitions are useful in more than one program file.

INITIALIZING STRUCTURES

We initialize structures in much the same way we initialized arrays, with initializer lists. Here we will declare a static occurrence of a 'diamond' and initialize it.

```
static diamond stone = { 12345L, 1, 4, .34 };
```

Because of the position of the numbers, 12345L has been assigned to 'stone.id_no', 1 to 'stone.color', and so on.

ARRAYS AND STRUCTURES

Since 'diamond' is now a data type, we should be allowed to create arrays of diamonds, as shown below:

```
struct diamond stones[15];
```

Now we want to get to the members of the elements of this array of 'diamonds'. To do this, just state the array name with subscript, then a '.' and the member name. Let's set the clarity of the seventh member of our array to 3.

```
stones[6].clarity = 3;
```

We can also initialize structure arrays by using what we've learned for both arrays and structures. Our initializer list for the array will contain several initializer lists for structures. Let's initialize a three-element array of diamonds.

```
static diamond stones[] =
            {
            { 3333L, 3, 4, 0.56 },
            { 4444L, 3, 3, 0.33 },
            { 5555L, 4, 2, 0.10 }
        };
```

POINTERS TO STRUCTURES

This is an especially useful combination and is very commonly used when passing information to functions or returning information from functions. We define a pointer to a structure by placing a '*' before the variable name.

```
struct diamond *gem_ptr;
```

There are two ways to access a member of a structure when we have only the pointer to the structure. One way is to enclose a '*' and the pointer name in parentheses, then list the member name (this must be done because of precedence).

```
(*gem_ptr).id_no = 17113L;
```

A special operator was developed to handle the situation of accessing a member when we have only the pointer, '->'. Using this operator, all we have to do is specify the pointer name, followed by '->', followed by the member name. This format is generally preferred to the one above. The following line is the exact equivalent of the statement above.

```
gem_ptr->id_no = 17113L;
```

FUNCTIONS AND STRUCTURES

It is important to know how to use structures and functions together because structures can make information handling within the program easier. We should know how to pass this information in structures to functions and also return this information from the function to the caller. In both cases there are two ways to do this: by using a pointer to a structure, or the structure itself. The pointer to a structure is often used in preference to the structure itself because it is usually more efficient. Remember that a structure may consist of hundreds of bytes, whereas most pointers are either two or four bytes.

We will illustrate the use of structures and functions by creating a function to price diamonds. The following formula is for demonstration purposes only and is not accurate. Our general formula for pricing diamonds will be:

```
PRICE = (1 + COLOR *.33) * ((1 + CLARITY * .40) * SIZE * 700)
```

We will pass the address of a diamond down to our function and it will return a float representing the price.

```
#define BASE 700.0
#define COL_FACTOR 0.33
#define CLAR_FACTOR 0.40

struct diamond {
                long id_no;
                int color;
                int clarity;
                float carats;
              };

float price( struct diamond *gem );

main()
{
    static struct diamond stone = { 12345L, 2, 3, .50 };
```

```
        printf("the diamond price for diamond  %ld is %f\n",
                    stone.id_no, price(&stone));
}

float price(struct diamond *gem)
{
    return ( ( 1 + gem->color * COL_FACTOR )   *
            ( 1 + gem->clarity * CLAR_FACTOR ) * gem->carats * BASE ) );
}
```

In the 'price()' function, because we used a pointer to structure instead of a structure, we had to use '->'. The only changes that would be necessary if we wanted to pass the structure instead of the pointer would be to define 'gem' as a structure rather than a pointer to a structure, and to replace all our '->' operators with the '.' operator.

We can also return structures or pointers to structures from functions. Let's write a program with a function that finds the most valuable diamond in an array of diamonds, and returns a pointer to this structure. We will pass an array of diamonds down and get back a pointer to the most valuable diamond.

Our function will be called 'best_stone()'. Now we have to define it as a function returning a pointer to a structure of type diamond. Therefore the first line of our function definition will be similar to the line below (note the '*' before our function name):

```
struct diamond *best_stone(...)
```

We will be receiving an array of diamond structures from the calling module and a count of the number of elements in the array. We use the same format as we used to pass arrays of simple variables (i.e., we don't have to declare the size of the array). The first line of our function definition now looks as below:

```
struct diamond *best_stone( int count, struct diamond gems[] )
```

The rest of the function is a little more straightforward except that we must declare a pointer to the highest diamond, and go through each diamond, calculating the price, then comparing that calculated price to the previous highest price, and resetting the highest price and the pointer to the highest price if necessary.

```
#define COL_FACTOR 0.33
#define CLAR_FACTOR 0.40
#define BASE 700.0

struct diamond {
                long id_no;
                int color;
                int clarity;
                float carats;
            };
float price( struct diamond *gem );
struct diamond *best_stone( int count, struct diamond gems[] );
```

```
main ()
{
    struct diamond *top_ice;
    static struct diamond stones[] = { { 12345L, 2, 3, .50 },
                                        { 25644L, 4, 4, .30 },
                                        { 33123L, 3, 1, .40 }
                                      };

    top_ice = best_stone(3, stones);
    printf("The most valuable diamond is %ld \n",
                top_ice->id_no, );
}

struct diamond *best_stone( int count, struct diamond gems[] )
{
    int i;
    float high_price = 0.0, value;
    struct diamond *best_diamond = gems;

    for ( i = 0; i < count; i++ )
    {
        if ( (value = price(&gems[i]) > high_price )
        { high_price = value;
            best_diamond = &gems[i];
        }
    }
    return ( best_diamond );
}

float price( struct diamond *gem )
{
    return ( (1 + gem->color * COL_FACTOR)    *
             (( 1 + gem->clarity * CLAR_FACTOR) * gem->carats * BASE) );
}
```

STRUCTURES WITHIN STRUCTURES

Once a structure has been defined, there is nothing to stop us from using it in the definition of other structures. Let's extend our structure definition of a diamond by including a purchase date. Since a date is a very useful entity on its own, we will set up a structure to describe it, then use that structure definition in defining a diamond.

```
struct date { int year;
              int mon;
              int day;
            };

struct diamond { long id_no;
                 int color;
                 int clarity;
                 float carats;
                 struct date purchase_date;
               } gem;
```

Now if we want to access the year of the purchase date, we will have to name the structure occurrence name, 'gem', then select the 'purchase_date' member using a '.', and further select the 'year' member of 'purchase_date' with another '.' We will set the year in our purchase date to 1989.

```
gem.purchase_date.year = 1989;
```

TYPEDEF AND STRUCTURES

typedef is a statement that is commonly associated with structures although it can be used with any type of data. typedef allows us to give our own special names to any data type. It will often make the program more easily read and more easily changed. To use typedef you just provide the data type you want renamed first, and the new name you want to use second. Although it is not mandatory, it is a convention to use uppercase letters whenever you define your own type. Now let's define a data type that could be used for variables that represent codes with a small set of possible values. We will actually represent it using an integer and call it 'CODE'.

```
typedef int CODE;
```

Now that we have a new data type, we can use it in other definitions or declarations. An example is shown below.

```
struct diamond {
            long id_no;
            CODE color;
            CODE clarity;
            float carats;
            };
```

If our diamond pricing program grew larger and we were very restricted for memory, we could now easily change our codes from integers to characters by just changing our typedef as shown below. We wouldn't have to search through our entire program looking for integers used for code-type variables.

typedef is commonly used with structure definitions. As before, you use the typedef keyword, then the data type, then the new name. This time, however, the data type will be a structure definition (without the template name or occurrence name). Let's use our diamond structure as an example.

```
typedef int CODE;

typedef struct {
            long id_no;
            CODE color;
            CODE clarity;
            float carats;
            } DIAMOND;
```

Now we can use DIAMOND wherever we used 'struct diamond' in the earlier part of the chapter. An example is shown below.

```
DIAMOND stones[3];
```

Much like structure definitions, any use of typedef is usually placed in a header file so that it can easily be incorporated into any program file in the program.

UNIONS

A union is very similar to a structure. The main difference is that the members of a union overlap the same area of memory, thereby saving space. It also allows us to interpret or redefine the same area of memory in several ways. Since the members overlap the same area of memory, if you set one member of the union you will alter the values of the other members of the union. This is one reason why it is not commonly used. A union definition follows the same format as a structure definition, and member access also follows the same pattern. An example of a union definition and member accesses are shown below.

```
union datum { int i_var;
              float f_var;
              char c_var;
            } info;

info.f_var = 4.700;
info.i_var = 121;

printf("the value of our float is %f\n", info.f_var);
```

In the code above we set the value of two members of our union. However, we can't know what we're going to get printed as a float. Integer 121 was placed in the same memory area as 'info.f_var' and a new pattern of bits was established for our `float`. When we go to print out our float, we get garbage.

ENUMERATED TYPES

An enumerated type is a way to give names to a sequence of integer-like constants. In some ways it works the same as using multiple `#define`'s to name all the numbers that occur in an expected set of values. It makes the program more readable and provides some protection by ensuring that only the proper constant names are assigned to any variable that is an enumerated type.

As a simple case, we will set up an enumerated type for the colors of the spectrum: red, orange, yellow, green, blue, indigo, and violet. Using `enum` also follows much the same pattern as defining and using structures. You use the `enum` keyword, then the enumerated type name (which is optional), then list the names for the constants of the enumerated type then, if necessary, the occurrence names. An example is shown below.

```
enum color { red, orange, yellow, green,
             blue, indigo, violet} laser, paint;
```

'color' is the template name, and 'laser' and 'paint' are actual occurrences of this type. We can assign any one of the constants to either 'laser' or 'paint'.

```
paint = yellow;
```

The compiler actually treats these enumerated types as a sequence of integers starting at zero (our colors would really be a sequence of integers starting from 0 and going to 6). In spite of this, they generally cannot be used as proper integers unless you cast them first (i.e., (int) laser). We can also force a specific value on any one of the constants, and elements following it will increase by one from the forced value.

```
enum color { red, orange = 5, yellow, green,
             blue = 14, indigo, violet };
```

STRUCTURES—A SYNOPSIS

What Are They?

Structures provide a method of grouping several individual data items under one name. The data items might be of different types.

What Are They Used For?

They help reduce the logical complexity of some problems. It means we can deal with a 'car' instead of the ten items necessary to describe the car. They also make it easier to pass complex but related sets of information to and from functions.

How Do You Declare a Structure?

Use the keyword struct, then, if necessary, the name of the conceptual template for the structure, then list all members necessary to make up one structure, and list the actual occurrence names.

```
struct diamond {
              long id_no;
              int color;
              int clarity;
              float carats;
          } hope, dust;
```

What Operators Do You Use?

Use '.' for member selection when you have an actual structure.

```
struct diamond hope;
hope.color = 3;
```

Use '->' for member selection when you are using a pointer to a structure instead of an actual structure.

```
struct diamond *struct_ptr;
struct_ptr = &hope;
struct_ptr->carats = .45;
```

PUTTING IT TOGETHER

POLLUTION ANALYSIS

Some trends in urban pollution can be determined from the weather records for the city or town. We will now use what we have learned about files, dynamic memory allocation, structure definitions, typedef, and enum to build a program that will do elementary analysis of weather and pollution over a city. The program will load an array of 'bad days' from a file containing daily weather records for that city. All the data in the file is stored in text format with each day's information on a separate line, and each unit of information (field) separated by blanks. Each city's information will be stored in a separate file.

The first step in this process is to design our data. We will establish which parameters are necessary to adequately record the daily weather information for the city then set up this description as a structure and a `typedef` in a separate header file, "weather.h". Structure definitions commonly go in their own header files because they will often be used by several files within a program. Notice that we used `enum` for our wind directions and precipitation types. The name we gave our data item is WEATHER_DAY.

The first thing our program will do is load an array of 'bad days' from our weather file using 'load_bad_days()'. We will load these structures only if the pollution exceeds a certain level. Since we will not know how many days we will have to load into our array, it is appropriate to use dynamic memory allocation. We will set up an array of pointers to WEATHER_DAY in 'analysis.c', then use 'load_bad.c' file to load the data. We will read the data into a WEATHER_DAY structure, and when we determine that it fits our criteria (pollution over a threshold), we will dynamically allocate a WEATHER_DAY structure, copy the information over from the automatic structure to the newly created structure (using structure assignment), and assign the address of this new structure to the next available location in the 'bad_days' array. We will use 'count' to keep track of how many bad days we have.

'load_bad_days()' must open the weather file initially and then read every record until the end of file is reached. It will return the count of the records loaded, or an error code. It will error check for an unsuccessful open of the file, an allocation error (e.g., not enough memory) and for an improper record (i.e., not enough data items on a line). We used negative numbers for our error codes because our 'count' should always be 0 or greater.

Because the data is stored in text format we could use `scanf()` or some version of it to convert the information. We will get a line at a time using `fgets()`. This will ensure that the bounds of our array, 'buffer', are not overshot and will also ensure that we process one single line at a time. This way we can test to see that the proper number of fields is on the line (11). We will use `sscanf()` to extract the information out of the string, and provide `sscanf()` with the buffer name, a conversion string, and the addresses of all the individual members of our WEATHER_DAY. `sscanf()` returns the number of successful conversions made so we can easily test to see that 11 conversions were made.

We will do a very simple analysis of the weather and pollution by analyzing wind speed as it relates to pollution. Once the array has been loaded with the information we will calculate some averages for different weather parameters and print out the results.

The program is assembled from five different files: two header files and three program files. "weather.h" contains structure definitions for weather information, "errors.h" defines error codes used in the program, "pollute.c" is the main driver of the program that loads the bad days then performs the analysis, "load_bad.c" loads information for any day over the pollution threshold from a file into a global array, and finally "analyze.c" performs the analysis on the data that has been loaded.

```
-----------------------------------------------------------------------
/* WEATHER.H   Type and structure definitions relating to
               weather information. */

#define DIRECTIONS 8
enum direction { N, NE, E, SE, S, SW, W, NW };

enum p_type { RAIN, SNOW, SLEET, HAIL, FREEZING_RAIN };
typedef struct { int year;
                 int month;
                 int day;
               } DATE;

typedef struct {
               DATE w_day;
               float mean_temp;
               int pollution_index;
               float rel_hum;
               float wind_speed;
               enum direction wind_dir;
               float precip;
               enum p_type precip_type;
               float precip_ph;
             } WEATHER_DAY;

-----------------------------------------------------------------------

/* ERRORS.H    Error codes for file and dynamic
               allocation errors.
*/
#define FILE_NOT_FOUND -1
#define ALLOCATION -2
#define RECORD_ERROR -3

-----------------------------------------------------------------------

/* POLLUTE.C  This program will load the daily weather information
              for days that exceed the pollution threshold into an
              array, then perform some elementary analyses on this
              data. The daily weather information is read in from a
              file. This file requires 'analysis()' (in ANALYZE.C)
              and 'load_bad_days()' (in LOAD_BAD.C ).
*/

#include <stdio.h>
#include "weather.h"
#include "errors.h"
#define MAX_DAYS 366
#define HEALTH_RISK 20

void analysis( int count );
int load_bad_days( char *city_code, int threshold );
```

```
WEATHER_DAY *bad_days[MAX_DAYS];
main()
{   int ret_value;
    char city[25];

    printf("\nPOLLUTION ANALYSIS");
    printf("\nEnter File Name for Analysis");
    scanf("%s", city );

    ret_value = load_bad_days( city, HEALTH_RISK );
    if ( ret_value == ALLOCATION )
        printf("not enough memory for program");
    else if ( ret_value == RECORD_ERROR )
        printf("improper record in the file");
    else if ( ret_value == FILE_NOT_FOUND )
        printf("could not open file");
    else
        analysis(ret_value);

}
```

```
/* LOAD_BAD.C   This file will load weather information for the days
                that exceed a pollution threshold into an external
                array of 'bad days'. The 'load_bad_days()' function
                will receive the name of the city file to process and
                the pollution threshold to compare against. It
                returns the count of records loaded or an error code
                (defined in "errors.h"). */

#include <stdio.h>
#include <stdlib.h>
#include "weather.h"
#include "errors.h"
#define BUF_LEN 101

extern WEATHER_DAY *bad_days[];

int load_bad_days( char *city_code, int threshold )
{
    FILE *infile;
    char buffer[BUF_LEN];
    WEATHER_DAY *p , this_day;
    int conversions;
    int count = 0;
    int out_of_data = 0;
    int error = 0;

    if ( (infile = fopen( city_code, "r")) == NULL )
        return ( FILE_NOT_FOUND );                /*** FUNCTION EXIT ***/
```

```
     while ( !out_of_data && !error )
     {
       if ( fgets( buffer, BUF_LEN, infile ) == NULL )
         out_of_data = 1;
       else
       {
         conversions = sscanf(buffer,
                           "%d%d%d%f%d%f%f%d%f%d%f",
                           &this_day.w_day.year,
                           &this_day.w_day.month,
                           &this_day.w_day.day,
                           &this_day.mean_temp,
                           &this_day.pollution_index,
                           &this_day.rel_hum,
                           &this_day.wind_speed,
                           &this_day.wind_dir,
                           &this_day.precip,
                           &this_day.precip_type,
                           &this_day.precip_ph);

         if( conversions != 11 )
           error = RECORD_ERROR;
         else if ( this_day.pollution_index >= threshold )
         {
           p = ( WEATHER_DAY *) malloc(sizeof(WEATHER_DAY ));
           if ( p == NULL )
             error = ALLOCATION;
           else
           {
             bad_days[count] = p;
             *bad_days[count] = this_day;
             count++;
           }
         }
       }
     }

  fclose(infile);
  if( error)
    return (error);
  else
    return (count);
}


------------------------------------------------------------------------


/* ANALYZE.C   This file does elementary analysis of the weather
               records loaded into 'bad_days'. It must receive the
               number of records to process.
*/

#include <stdio.h>
#include "weather.h"

extern WEATHER_DAY *bad_days[];
```

```
void analysis( int count )
{
    int i;
    float total_index = 0.0;
    float total_ph = 0.0;
    float total_wind_speed = 0.0;

    for( i = 0; i < count; i++ )
    {
        total_ph += bad_days[i]->precip_ph;
        total_index += bad_days[i]->pollution_index;
        total_wind_speed += bad_days[i]->wind_speed;
    }

    printf("number of bad days  %d\n", count);
    printf("average pollution index on bad days %f\n",
                    total_index / count);
    printf("average wind speed %f\n", total_wind_speed / count);
    printf("average pH of precipitation  %f\n", total_ph / count);
}
```

LABORATORY 10

1. Define a structure to represent a point on a grid. It should have an 'x' co-ordinate and a 'y' co-ordinate, both of which are floats.

2. Write a function that receives two 'point' structures representing the top left and bottom right corner of a rectangle and returns a float representing the area of the rectangle. The formula for area is Length x Width. Alter your code so that it receives two pointers to 'point' instead of the actual structure.

3. Using our previous definition of a 'point', how would you represent a circle as a simple structure? Write a function that receives a pointer to a circle and returns a double representing the area (3.14159 * radius * radius). Change the program so that you use a typedef for 'point'.

4. Write a function that receives two 'point' structures representing the top left and bottom right corner of a rectangle and returns a pointer to a circle structure representing the largest circle that will fit inside that rectangle.

5. Define a structure called 'flight' that contains

flight number	– 10 characters
orig	– 20 characters
destination	– 20 characters
arrival	– structure time
departure	– structure time
time zones	– float

Time zones is the difference in time zones between the origin and destination. It is positive if destination is west of the origin, and negative if destination is east of the origin. 'time' is a structure that is composed of 'hour' (integer), and 'min' (integer). The 'hour' figure uses a 24-hour clock.

Write a program that allows the user to load an array of 'flights' and finds the shortest and longest flight duration.

6. Enhance the analysis function of the Pollution Analysis program by analyzing and displaying the most common wind directions on the polluted days. (NOTE: Enumerated types such as those used in the example behave as integers.)

11
FINE TUNING

Now that we have acquired a reasonable grasp of programming in C, we can look at more difficult questions. The topics we will discuss in this chapter are: when to use C instead of another language, writing efficient code, writing portable code, and suggestions for further study in C.

WHY USE C ?

Once you become proficient in C, there might be a temptation to write all your code in C. Before you give in to this temptation, always evaluate its strengths against its weaknesses. For some applications, it might be wise to use higher-level languages.

C is often chosen as an implementation language because:

- It produces fast and compact object code.
- It allows us to write portable programs.
- It allows access to the machine with bit operators.
- It allows us to easily write structured solutions.

Because C is elegant and simple it allows the programmer both flexibility and power in solving problems that would be tricky in other languages. It is used for graphics, all sorts of micro applications (many of the most popular micro spreadsheets and databases are written in C), file utilities, process control, robotics, and real time processing.

There are many applications for which C could do the job but other languages might be better suited. For any problem, you should choose a language that allows you to concentrate on the conceptual solution to the problem and that makes the implementation of that solution as transparent as possible. Other important factors are ease of maintenance, ease of understanding, and portability.

Whether or not to use C is a judgment call. An example is a mainframe data processing environment. These systems are often quite large, many people are involved in their maintenance and development, and they are often altered because of changing specifications. Here a high-level database language or COBOL might be preferable because the English-like syntax and high-level commands allow an easier understanding of the problem and therefore should allow quicker changes. C could be used effectively in these systems by having COBOL or the database control the system, and have C subroutines to do the 'dirty work'.

One other example is artificial intelligence. There are many languages specially designed to deal with one problem area. These languages come with complicated built-in mechanisms to solve problems of a specific type. For instance, PROLOG, an artificial intelligence language, comes with built-in mechanisms that allow the programmer to make suppositions and to search suppositions to find one that is true. The programmer has been saved from this work and can concentrate on setting up the proper logical relationships instead of designing efficient search routines.

EFFICIENCY

We will look at several points regarding efficiency. The best technique at improving efficiency is to choose or design an efficient algorithm. This judgment cannot be taught in a workbook. There are, however, some easily applied techniques to improve efficiency.

Use the Correct Data type
Integer arithmetic is more efficient than floating point arithmetic. If possible, declare numeric data as integers. In older compilers, floating point arithmetic and the passing of data to functions is always done using `doubles`. That means that if you use a `float`, it must be changed to a `double` before any operation can be done. If you must use a fractional number on these compilers, and space is less important than speed (`doubles` take more space than `floats`), always use `double`.

Use Library Functions
Using library functions is advisable because they are usually more portable and are often designed to be efficient. They are also efficient with respect to programmer time—if the right function is in the library, you won't have to design, code or test it.

Prudent Use of Formatted Input/Output
`scanf()` and `printf()` are very powerful functions but can be inefficient. These functions must interpret your format string before they can do any real work. You can do any necessary format conversions by using `getchar()` or `putchar()` and one of the many conversion functions in the standard library. These functions convert strings to the different numeric data types and vice versa.

Using Macros
Using functions for a small amount of code such as a single line is not efficient because of the calling mechanism used in C. A way to replace these

small functions is by writing a macro, using `#define`.

A macro is similar, in some ways, to a function, but unlike a function a macro is not called. Before our program is compiled all the statements that make up the macro are substituted into our source code wherever the macro name is used. We have already seen the `#define`, which we used to substitute a string such as QUIT by a string '99', and we will use `#define` to write our macros.

Let's look at the task of taking the absolute value of any number. The code for this is very short.

```
absvalue = ( x < 0 )? -x : x;
```

It would not be wise to do this using a function because of the amount of overhead associated with calling functions. It would also be cumbersome to have to rewrite this code every time we wished to find an absolute value. The solution is to write a macro under the name of `abs` which will automatically substitute this code wherever `abs` is used within the program. We should put these macros at the top of the program with the `#define`s.

```
#define abs(x)  ( (x) < 0 ? -(x):(x) )
```

Now within our program we could use 'abs' as if it were a function, although all the code necessary to do the task is being duplicated every time we wish to use it.

The following code

```
q = abs(rndnum);
```

is actually expanded to

```
q = ((rndnum<0)?-(rndnum):(rndnum));
```

by the preprocessor before compilation takes place. Please note that in our original macro definition we did not include the ";", because it would have been substituted into our code, and we would have had an extra ";" in our statement.

In our macro definition, we also bracketed the 'variable' part of the definition (i.e., 'x'). In fact, there are a lot of brackets in our macro definition. This relates to the fact that a macro might be used in a complex statement and we want to ensure that all operations are done in the proper order, and also because we can expect expressions as arguments to a macro. Let's set up a simple macro that squares a number or expression and see what happens when we leave out the brackets. The definition of our macro is as follows:

```
/*  this macro definition is error-prone !!  */
#define square(x)  x * x
```

Now see what happens if we try to use the macro as follows.

```
result = square(7 + 3)/5.0;
```

Although we would expect 'result' to be 20, it actually becomes 28.6 because the statement above is expanded as below:

```
result = 7 + 3 * 7 + 3/5.0;
```

If we had defined our macro properly as follows:

```
#define square(x)  ((x) * (x))
```

our expanded code would look as below and produce the proper results:

```
result = ((7 + 3) * (7 + 3))/5.0;
```

The abs macro described above can be found in "stdlib.h" in ANSI compilers and in 'stdio.h' in older compilers, so it can be used any time you include the appropriate header file in your program.

PORTABILITY

Although C can be used to write programs that run on more than one machine, it can't be done without careful attention by the programmer. Since the subject of portability is large (it could fill a book), we will briefly discuss three points:

- the portability of code (general)
- the portability of interface code
- the portability of data

Portability of Code—General

As a general rule, C programs are portable if: only the standard C syntax is used; the only library function calls are from the standard library; and no machine-specific code using bit operators or absolute addresses are used. One possible problem with porting these programs is the int data type. On large machines, the 'int' data range is usually from -2,147,483,648 to 2,147,483,647 whereas on the PC the range for integer data is -32768 to 32767. This could cause problems if you are porting from the large machine to the PC.

This tells us that, if possible, we should stay away from 'compiler-specific' functions that come only with the compiler used, function libraries that are not portable themselves, and from bit operators. Unfortunately, this isn't always possible.

We want to use purchased and free-ware function libraries to cut down on our programming time. There is no point in reinventing the wheel. We should choose these libraries on three factors: quality, price, and the target machines they work on. This could mean choosing a good library that works on four machines over an excellent library that works on only one. Several of the computer magazines commonly review function libraries.

What if we must write machine-specific code? C allows us to write programs in separate 'source files', compile them separately, then link the generated object files into one program. If we put all the machine-specific code into one source file, we will have to change only one file instead of several when we move the application to a new machine.

Another technique used to handle machine-specific code is conditional compilation. We can write our program so that parts of the code will be compiled only if a certain symbol has been defined using a #define. This means we can put code in the program for every machine we wish the program to run on, and by defining the appropriate symbol (e.g., #define VAX) only one part of the code is compiled. The preprocessor statements that allow this conditional compilation are listed below.

#if SYMBOL1	'has SYMBOL1 been equated with a non-zero value'
#ifdef SYMBOL1	'has SYMBOL1 been defined at all'
#else	'do when #if or #ifdef above it isn't true'
#elif SYMBOL2	'test SYMBOL2 if first condition isn't true'
#endif	'end the conditional block.' You must have this in every conditional block.
#undef SYMBOL1	'undefine SYMBOL1 for the rest of the program'. Preprocessor will now treat SYMBOL1 as if it had never been defined.

Now let's look at our integer problem and solve it two ways using conditional compilation. We will first set up a separate one-line header file, 'machine.h', which will tell our compiler what type of machine we are working with. In this case, we will set it up for a VAX.

```
#define VAX
```

Note that we didn't assign any replacement value to the symbol VAX. At the top of our program we will include this machine header.

```
#include "machine.h"
```

Now, somewhere within our code we are going to test if the machine is a PC, and define a variable 'number' as a long int or int depending on machine type.

```
#ifdef PC
    long int number;
#else
    int number;
#endif
```

The #ifdef checks if the symbol 'PC' has been defined using a #define. Since this symbol hasn't been defined, the code following the #else is compiled. We could have accomplished the same result using #if, but we would have to change our header, "machine.h".

```
#define PC 0
```

We would change the code within our program to:

```
#if PC
    long int number;
#else
    int number;
#endif
```

The #if tests the symbol 'PC' to see if it has been equated with a non-zero value. Because 'PC' is 0, it automatically goes to the #else. Note that these conditional blocks can be placed anywhere within our program.

Portable Interfaces

Writing for a portable interface is a very difficult problem since there are so many terminal and monitor types. One solution is to choose screen and window libraries that work on as many devices as possible. One screen library, "curses", has become a standard on UNIX machines. It is now migrating to other machines (including the PC) and can be used with all sorts of terminals.

There are also window management standards being developed that promise to be very portable. Another alternative is to use the sophisticated screen management libraries that run on micros, minis and mainframes.

Another technique for relatively portable text-oriented interfaces is to use ANSI escape sequences. The PC and any terminal that is compatible with a VT-100 or higher series (there are a lot of them out there) can be set to respond to these sequences. These escape sequences can be used to do such things as clear the screen, move the cursor, and set scrolling regions. An escape sequence usually consists of the escape character (ASCII character 27 or '\033'), the '[', and a command string. For instance, the escape sequence to clear the screen is <escape>[2J. Once our terminal has been set up as an ANSI device, we can clear the screen using either of the following two lines.

```
printf("\033[2J");
putchar('\033'); putchar('['); putchar('2'); putchar('J');
```

Direct cursor addressing is achieved by the escape sequence <escape>[lineno;columnoH. Let's move the cursor to line 10 and column 20.

```
printf("\033[10;20H");
```

Any terminal manual will list all the valid ANSI escape sequences. Investigate the ANSI escape sequences by setting a scrolling region on the screen.

Portable Data

The portability of data is more important than portability of code since the data might be used by other (non-C) applications on a variety of machines. In many cases, the solution is very simple—use a sequential, pure ASCII file with fixed-length fields. Left-pad all your numeric fields with zeros. If you wish to use `fscanf()` you might want to separate your fields with blanks. This simple technique will allow your data to be easily read by other languages on PCs or mainframes, by LOTUS 1-2-3, wordprocessors, and databases such as dBASE.

THE NEXT STEP

This workbook was designed to allow a user to quickly attain a working proficiency in C. Although the commands and operators discussed in this book should allow you to tackle a large majority of the problems you will encounter, your study of C should not stop here. Listed below are some suggested subject areas for investigation and experimentation:

- Learning how to use a variety of libraries.
- More sophisticated use of pointers (e.g., pointers to functions, functions returning pointers, pointers to pointers, tables of pointers, etc.).
- Recursion (writing functions that call themselves).
- Using structures, pointers, and dynamic memory allocation to implement linked lists.
- Developing multiple file programs (where source code resides on several text files).
- Experimentation with operators.
- File handling using low-level input and output functions.

LABORATORY 11

1. Write a macro that will give the area of circle when given the radius. Test it with the following numbers and expressions;

   6

   6+7

   x (an integer variable)

2. Write a macro, 'max', to return the larger of two numbers.

3. VAXPF1, VAXPF2, PCF1, PCF2 have been defined as valid symbols using '#define'. VAXPF1 and VAXPF2 work only on a VAX and PCF1 and PCF2 work only on a PC. Using conditional compilation, rewrite the following code so that only the appropriate part of the code will be compiled depending on whether the symbols VAX or PC have been defined.

```
response = getkey();              /*   assume 'getkey()' is already
                                                   written   */
switch (response)
{
   case '1'      : option_1();
                   break;
   case '2'      : option_2();
                   break;
   case VAXPF1   :
   case PCF1     : help();
                   break;
   case VAXPF2   :
   case PCF2     : recall();
                 : break;
   default       : input_error();
                   break;
}
```

12

CASE STUDY— A DIAMOND PRICING SYSTEM

A GLIMPSE AT THE BIG PICTURE

We have looked at many features of C and should now be able to tackle larger programs. Unfortunately, there is a significant difference between developing small programs and large programs. It is neither very costly nor difficult to change a small program. It can be costly or even impossible to change a large program safely. The consequences of bugs or poor design are magnified in large programs. They will often affect 1000 or 2000 lines of code instead of 40. Because of these two facts, we must approach large program design with particular care.

The first step when faced with larger programs is to shift our concentration from writing code to design. We have to look at the features of the job and not concentrate on the many tasks that make up the job. We must also consider the possibility of future changes (this is almost a certainty). We also want to build a robust program in which the effect of a bug is localized and therefore easy to find and change. Making sure that we have good internal documentation is now even more important. Often even the creator of a large program has difficulty understanding it after not working on it for a short time.

One technique we will use is to split our programs into several program files. The reasoning here is that since we were able to write and test small programs without too much difficulty, why not create our large programs from several small programs. Program files aren't really programs but they can be compiled separately and allow us to protect or hide data inside the file from the outside world (other program files). After we have finished writing and compiling all program files we can link all the objects created by compiling into an executable (runnable) program. Only one of our program files is allowed to have a `main()` function, however.

Up to this point in the book we have been mainly concerned with one question in writing our programs: "How do we do it?"

Once we answered this, we turned all the tasks necessary to complete the job into functions. We designed the functions as black boxes whenever possible. Now in addition to the question above, we have to look at other important questions such as: (i) "How do we describe our data?" and (ii) "How do we arrange the program code into different program files?"

The proper description of data could seriously affect the overall simplicity of the system (a very important factor in performance, maintenance, and ease of understanding). How we divide the program into files will affect the ease with which the program can be changed or refined.

LARGE SYSTEM DEVELOPMENT

The development of large systems is an involved process that includes determining the user's true needs, delivering a product (a software system), setting up the mechanisms for enhancement of the system, correcting bugs, and if necessary, training the users. We will develop a simple system that will deal with the needs of small jewelry stores. This system will be designed with a view to allowing future enhancements and making the program easy to use.

The fields of Systems Analysis and Systems Design deal with the concepts and techniques for developing and maintaining large systems. Since we cannot cover such broad areas of study in this book, we will choose one sequence of steps to develop our system and explain our reasoning. It is important to note that there are often several approaches that can be taken in the development of systems. The sequence of steps we will take is listed below.

1. Evaluate the user's needs. If possible get an understanding of the user's business and establish priorities (i.e., What is needed first?).

2. Develop an overview of the system.

3. Design the primary data.

4. Design overall program structure and identify any toolboxes needed. At this point acquire or build the necessary toolboxes.

5. Write the remaining modules starting from the top down.

Business Background

A major part of business for jewelry stores is the sale of small 'brilliant' diamonds of a carat or less. Although most other gems (including large diamonds) are hard to price except by experts, these small diamonds can be easily priced by using a pricing table or grid. Considerable time could be saved for the jeweler if we could develop a system that would automate this pricing and provide an accounting of inventory.

There are several features of small diamonds and gems in general that must be considered before we design our system. First, diamond prices change frequently, mainly because of market pressures. Second, diamond prices change in an irregular manner. For instance, one size range or color may change, without any others being affected. Finally there are four main factors that describe a diamond and therefore influence its price:

- shape
- clarity
- color
- size

System Overview

Based on our initial assessment of user needs, we have decided that we should develop an easy-to-use menu-driven system for both diamond pricing and inventory in small- and medium-sized jewelry stores. Although these are the only functions we will look at initially, it is likely that further enhancements or functions will be required later. We must be careful not to "box ourselves in" with our initial design. The client is most interested in the automated pricing system and can wait for the full-blown inventory control system.

Our program is going to be a simple menu-driven program that will initially calculate diamond prices only for diamonds between 0.0 and 1.0 carats but will eventually include inventory reporting and inquiries. The pricing will be accomplished using a regularly updated file of prices. A rough diagram of our program is shown below.

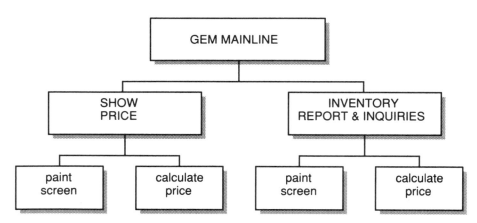

Now that we know what we have to do, we can concentrate on designing our more important data and 'filling out' our rough design. We will use a combination of top-down and bottom-up design to design our programs.

Data Design

The most important data item in our system is a diamond. We will design a data item that can adequately describe a diamond and other types of stones. We already know that the important features that describe a diamond are color, size, shape, and clarity. We will also need an identifier or number to uniquely identify each gem and a code to tell what type of gem it is. We will also need to store a cost price and a market price.

Now we can create a header file called "gems.h", which will contain a structure definition for a gem and symbolic names for each type of clarity, color, shape and gem type. We must assign codes where necessary and decide on the member data types for our gem structure. This isn't easy. Sometimes we have to decide on difficult compromises between efficient use of space and ease of processing.

This is how we will design our gem structure and our reasoning. We will use a long integer for the identifier because of the great range of values it can represent. We can use either a `char` or `int` to represent color, shape, clarity, and gem type. We will use an `int` in each case because, since `int` is the standard data type for C, it has a wider range (even though it isn't necessary), and is processed efficiently. We would have used a `char` if we had wanted to save space. We will use a `float` for both the cost price and market price.

Since this structure will be commonly used in our system we will establish it as a new type using `typedef`. The new type will be called GEM (upper case is commonly used for any user defined types).

Now we can set up our header file to contain the above information.

```
/* GEM.H   This file contains some global symbol
            definitions useful throughout program and
            the type definition for a "GEM".
*/

#define ERRLINE 24
#define ERRCOL 35
#define TRUE 1
#define FALSE 0

typedef struct   { long id_no;
                    int type;
                    int quality;
                    int color;
                    int shape;
                    float size;
                    float cost;
                    float market;
                 } GEM;
```

PROGRAM DESIGN

Now we must make an overall design for our programs. We have two ways of doing this. Top-down design involves taking our job and successively dividing it into smaller tasks until they can easily be encoded into functions. Bottom-up design involves identifying sets of primitive tools needed to complete the job, then building the program from these toolboxes. In fact, we will use both techniques in developing our program.

We have already used a little bit of top-down design in the rough design stage mentioned in the System Overview. With our rough design worked out, we should identify any tool sets that might be necessary. We might have to build these tool sets ourselves, but with luck they might be purchased for a reasonable price or might already be available on our system. From our initial diagram it is apparent that we will definitely need a set of screen-handling functions. These libraries of screen-handling functions are so commonly used that they are often found on both large and small systems (e.g., curses, a set of utility functions commonly found on UNIX systems). There is a wide variety of screen libraries available for microcomputers. It is usually wiser to acquire and use one of these libraries, because the work of coding and testing is already done for you and very often these functions have been optimized so that they are very efficient.

Toolbox 1

We are going to build a toolset of very basic screen instructions because the readers of this book are probably on a variety of machines and a toolset based on the ANSI escape sequences will work on many terminals (VT-100s and compatibles) as well as the PC. Furthermore, it's both simple and free of charge. All we have to do is decide on the primitive screen functions we need, then look up the appropriate escape sequences and create macros to print these escape sequences to the screen. The basic screen primitives we will use are:

1. Set the cursor at a given location.

2. Display a string at a given location.

3. Clear the screen.

4. Clear to end of line.

5. Turn BOLD attribute on.

6. Turn INVERSE attribute on.

7. Turn NORMAL attribute on.

We will place all these macros in a header file called "ansi.h". It is listed below.

```
/* ANSI.H   This file contains macros that will perform
            basic screen handling functions using the ANSI
            escape sequences.  These will work only if the
            display device is configured as an ANSI device.
*/

#define cls()      printf("\033[2J")
#define curset(r,c)  printf("\033[%d;%dH",(r),(c))
#define atsay(r,c,str) printf("\033[%d;%dH%s",(r),(c),(str))
#define bold()     printf("\033[1m")
#define reverse()  printf("\033[7m")
#define normal()   printf("\033[0m")
```

Toolbox 2

Part of developing good toolboxes is identifying commonly used activities and developing very general, reusable units to perform these tasks. Our original system design indicated that we would have to paint both menus and forms and get data or commands from these forms. We could develop a more sophisticated set of tools (which uses primitives from the first toolbox) that will deal with painting screens and perhaps getting data.

Before we start we should have an understanding of what a screen is. For our purposes, we could define a screen as a collection of display fields and input fields. We should be able to simplify part of the screen-handling process by defining a display field and an input field and setting up functions to handle these.

Our display field could be adequately described by the following:

1. A row position.

2. A column position.

3. An attribute (e.g., BOLD, NORMAL, etc).

4. A string to be displayed.

Our input fields are a little more complicated. Since we will be using them to get information from the screen, we will need a row and column position. However, since a user might make a mistake while entering any field, we will also need the location on the screen to display the error message. We should also know how large the input area should be. In other words, our structure should contain the following:

1. A row position.
2. A column position.
3. A field length.
4. A row position for the error message.
5. A column position for the error message.

We will define our display field and input fields as structures and set them off in a separate header file called "screen.h". Just as we did with the 'GEM' structure, we will establish these structures as types by using `typedef`. We should also use a few `#defines` to assign symbolic names to our attribute codes and any necessary declarations for the functions that will be contained in "screen.c". We will be creating several screen and input functions, so we will declare them here, since this file will be included whenever these functions are used. The functions are declared external because they will reside on another 'source file'. Our attribute codes will be 1 for NORMAL, 2 for BOLD, and 3 for REVERSE. The header file "screen.h" is listed below.

```
/* SCREEN.H  This header file contains definitions needed
             for the menu and form painting functions.*/

#define NORMAL 1
#define BOLD 2
#define REVERSE 3

typedef struct   { int row;
                    int col;
                    int att;
                    char *str;
                 } DISPLAY_FLD;

typedef struct   { int row;
                    int col;
                    int width;
                    int errlin;
                    int errcol;
                 } INPUT_FLD;

extern int get_int( INPUT_FLD *field, int high_value,
                    int low_value, int special );
extern float get_float( INPUT_FLD *field, float high_value,
                        float low_value, float special );
extern void put_screen( DISPLAY_FLD scr[] );
```

Now that we have defined a display field and an input field, we can start writing functions that will paint our screens and get data from the screen. We will set up all our screens as collections (arrays) of display fields. In order to display a screen, our function must receive an array of display fields. Since screens might have a variable number of fields, we will signal the end of our screen by setting the last display field to all NULL's or 0's. An example of setting up a screen using this technique is shown below.

```
static DISPLAY_FLD example[] =
   {
     { 7, 3, BOLD, "THIS IS ON LINE 7, AND BOLD" },
     { 15, 35, NORMAL, "THIS IS ON LINE 15 AND NORMAL" },
     { NULL, NULL, NULL, NULL }
   };
```

Now that we know how our screens are going to be set up, we can develop a 'put_screen()' function that receives an array of display fields and displays each field at its proper location with its proper attribute. In other words, we will be able to display a screen by simply passing an array name down to our 'put_screen()' function. The code for 'put_screen()' is shown below.

```
/* SCREEN.C  This file contains functions to display a screen
             from an array of display fields, and to get and
             validate either integers or floats from the screen.*/

#include <stdio.h>
#include <stdlib.h>
#include "ansi.h"
#include "screen.h"
#define TRUE 1
#define FALSE 0

void put_screen( DISPLAY_FLD scr[] )
{
  int i;
  normal();
  cls();
  for ( i=0; scr[i].row != NULL; i++ )
  { if ( scr[i].att == BOLD )
      bold();
    else if( scr[i].att == REVERSE )
      reverse();
    else
      normal();

    curset(scr[i].row, scr[i].col);
    puts(scr[i].str);
  }
  normal();
}
```

Getting and validating a field is considerably more difficult than simply painting a screen. Remember that we must get this choice from the right location on the screen, and if it is incorrect, display an error message. You may want to accept different types of data from different locations. In addition you might want to perform different tests to validate the field. The pseudocode outlined below shows a typical approach to data entry from screens.

VALIDATING AN INPUT FIELD

```
        SET valid-flag TO "no"
        CLEAR ERROR-AREA ON SCREEN

        DO WHILE valid-flag EQUAL TO "no"
            CLEAR INPUT-AREA ON SCREEN
            SET CURSOR
            GET user-entry
            VALIDATE user-entry
            IF user-entry IS VALID
                SET valid-flag TO "yes"
            ELSE
                DISPLAY ERROR MESSAGE AT ERROR LOCATION
            END-IF
        END-DO

        RETURN user-entry
```

One of the most common validations is to check that a number is within a certain range of numbers. Very often a special value outside this range is also allowed to signify a 'quit' condition or 'panic button'. We will write a function that will get a valid integer when it's sent a pointer to an 'INPUT_FLD', the high end of its allowed range, the low end of its allowed range, and any allowed value outside this range.

```
static INPUT_FLD i_field = { 10, 20, 8, 24, 30 };
int command;
command = get_int(&i_field, 5, 1, 99);
```

This code will keep attempting to get an eight-byte string ('width' member of our structure 'i_field') from location 10,20 on the screen, and validate that the integer is between 1 and 5 or else a special value 99. If we didn't want a special value, we could assign this member a value somewhere inside the range. The code for 'get_int()' is listed below.

```
int get_int( INPUT_FLD *field, int high_value,
             int low_value, int special)
{
   char reply[25];
   int rtnval, i, valid = FALSE;

   curset(field->errlin, field->errcol);
   cleol();

   while( !valid)
   {
      normal();
      curset(field->row, field->col);
      for ( i=0; i < field->width; i++ )
         putchar(' ');
      curset(field->row, field->col);
      gets(reply);
      rtnval = atoi(reply);
```

```
      if( (rtnval >= low_value && rtnval <= high_value) ||
            rtnval == special )
      valid = TRUE;
   else
   {
      bold();
      curset(field->errlin, field->errcol);
      printf("enter a number between %d and %d",
              low_value, high_value);
      if( special <low_value || special > high_value)
         printf(" or %d", special);
   }
}
   return (rtnval);
}
```

Please note that a different function would have to be written to accept floats (i.e., 'get_float()') but the only changes would be to redefine the function to return a float; redefine 'rtnval','high_value','low_value', and 'special' as floats and use atof() instead of atoi() to convert our string.

Toolbox 3

The last toolbox we will look at is one strictly devoted to calculating the price of a diamond. We will set this up as a separate toolbox because it will be used by several parts of the system. Also, since the method of pricing is likely to be changed and refined over the lifetime of the system, we should keep this part of the program relatively independent.

Prices will be calculated by searching a two-dimensional pricing array that has been loaded from a file. An example of a pricing table or array for diamonds is shown below. The rows of our array will represent the size range (between 0.0 and 1.0 carat) and the columns will represent the quality of the diamond (1 for VERY SLIGHT IMPERFECTIONS, 2 for SLIGHT IMPERFECTIONS, 3 for IMPERFECT, and 4 for REJECT). The first column of our array will represent the bottom end of the size range that corresponds to that row. An example array is shown below.

Size	Quality			
	Very Slight	Slight	Imperfect	Reject
.85	2800.00	2200.00	1500.00	700.00
.70	2200.00	1900.00	1350.00	700.00
.50	1800.00	1600.00	1200.00	600.00
.40	1600.00	1400.00	1000.00	530.00
.28	1400.00	1200.00	900.00	500.00
.23	1200.00	1000.00	800.0	450.00
.18	900.00	800.00	600.00	370.00
.14	700.00	650.00	540.00	340.00
.07	650.00	600.00	450.00	280.00
.00	600.00	540.00	440.00	260.00

The functions we will need to calculate prices are:

1. loadprices(): This will load the two-dimensional array from a file. It should return an error code if the load is unsuccessful.

2. price(): This will receive a pointer to a gem structure and returns the calculated price if the diamond is under one carat. It returns a negative value if an error has occurred (size out of range, or improper clarity).

```c
/* PRICE.C  This file contains the functions to load the
            pricing table for the diamonds and to price
            diamonds based on size and quality only.
*/

#include <stdio.h>
#include "gem.h"

#define ROWS 10
#define COLUMNS 5
#define ARRAY_FILE "price.dat"

static float prices[ROWS][COLUMNS];

int loadprices( void )
{
    FILE *price_file;
    int i, j, converts;
    int valid = TRUE;

    if ( (price_file = fopen(ARRAY_FILE, "r")) == NULL )
    { printf(" \cannot open %s", ARRAY_FILE);
      return ( NULL );
    }
    for ( i = 0; i < ROWS && valid == TRUE; i++ )
      for ( j = 0; j < COLUMNS && valid == TRUE; j++ )
        if ( (converts = fscanf(price_file, "%f", &(prices[i][j])))
                      == NULL )
            valid = FALSE;

    fclose(price_file);
    return ( valid );
}

float find_price( GEM *stone )
{
  int i;
  if ( stone->size > 1.0 || stone->size <= 0.0 )
    return ( -1.0 );

  if ( stone->quality < 1 || stone->quality > 4 )
    return ( -1.0 );

  for ( i = 0; stone->size < prices[i][0]; i++ )
    ;                           /* NULL BODY */
  return ( prices[i][stone->quality] );
}
```

BOTTOM-UP PROGRAMMING—A SUMMARY

We have just finished building the three toolsets we considered necessary for our system. The point you should have noticed is that we tried to make the individual tools (functions or macros) as general as possible so that they could be reused elsewhere. It might have seemed like too much work since our program presently will only calculate a diamond price. This ignores the fact that in the future we will have to use all of these same functions and macros in the components of the system that must be added later. Furthermore, our screen functions and macros are general enough so that we could use them in the interactive programs we write for several computer systems.

WORKING TOP-DOWN

Now that we have developed most of the necessary tools we can design and code the rest of the program.

Gem Mainline

This is the main driver for the entire program. It will first load the pricing array, then repeatedly paint the main menu, accept a choice from the user, and call the appropriate function until the user enters a special quit code. The pseudocode for this part of the program is shown below.

Pseudocode for Mainline of GEM.C

```
MAINLINE

    LOAD PRICE TABLE

    DO
       PAINT MAIN SCREEN
       GET VALID user-choice
       IF user-choice NOT EQUAL QUIT
           CALL APPROPRIATE FUNCTION
       END-IF
    WHILE user-choice NOT EQUAL TO QUIT

    DISPLAY ENDING MESSAGE
    END PROGRAM
```

```
/* GEM.C    This is the mainline for our gem pricing and inventory
            system. This module calls a module to load a pricing
            array and generates the main menu.
*/
#include <stdio.h>
#include "ansi.h"
#include "screen.h"
#include "gem.h"
#define INVENT 2
#define PRICES 1
#define QUIT 99

void show_price( void );
void inventory( void );

main()
{
   int choice;
   int successful_load;
   static DISPLAY_FLD  main_screen[] =

      { { 6, 18, REVERSE, "   GEM    PRICING    SYSTEM   "},
        { 10, 20, NORMAL, "1.  Calculate Diamond Price"},
        { 11, 20, NORMAL, "2.  Inventory Report"},
        { 13, 20, NORMAL, "99. QUIT Program"},
        { 16, 21, NORMAL, "ENTER CHOICE: "},
        { NULL, NULL, NULL, NULL }
      };

   static INPUT_FLD command ={ 16, 36, 10, ERRLINE, ERRCOL };

   if ( (successful_load = loadprices()) != TRUE )
   {
     cls();
     atsay(5,5,"ERROR occurred loading the price file");
     exit(1);
   }
   do {
        put_screen(main_screen);
        choice = get_int(&command, 2, 1, 99);

        if( choice == PRICES )
          show_price();
        else if ( choice == INVENT )
          inventory();
      } while ( choice != QUIT );

   cls();
   atsay(5, 5, "Have a nice day!");
}
```

Invent Module

This module will contain a stub. A stub is a function that performs no real work. We know that we don't have to finish this module until Version 1.1, so that if the user selects this option we will just display a message indicating that it's coming in the future. The code is listed below.

```
/* INVENT.C   Program stub for INVENTORY module.  */

#include <stdio.h>
#include "screen.h"

void inventory( void )
{
    char reply [25];
    static DISPLAY_FLD inventory[] =
    {
       { 3, 3, REVERSE, "   GEM      PRICING     SYSTEM   " },
       { 5, 3, NORMAL, " INVENTORY REPORTING SYSTEM" },
       { 6, 3, NORMAL, "This will be available in VERSION 1.1" },
       { 9, 3, NORMAL, "PRESS RETURN TO CONTINUE" },
       { NULL, NULL, NULL, NULL }
    };

    put_screen(inventory);
    gets(reply);
}
```

The 'show_price' Module

The 'show_price()' function displays an input form, gets and validates any necessary data to calculate a diamond price, and displays the price. If for some reason it cannot calculate the price, it will display an error message. Now, because we have already set up the necessary tools, coding this module is not too difficult. We will define our screen and input fields using the structures we have already set up, then use the functions in 'screen.c' to display our screen and get the data. Then we will use the function 'find_price()' in 'price.c' to calculate our price.

```
/* SHOW_PRC.C  This module displays a screen, gets both a  diamond
                size and quality, and displays its price.
*/

#include <stdio.h>
#include "gem.h"
#include "ansi.h"
#include "screen.h"

extern float find_price( GEM *stone );

void show_price( void )
{
    float price, size;
    char reply [25];
    int quality;
    GEM diamond;
```

```
static DISPLAY_FLD price_form[] =
{ { 5, 3, REVERSE,  "  GEM    PRICING      SYSTEM  " },
  { 7, 3, NORMAL,   " DIAMOND PRICING MODULE" },
  { 9, 3, NORMAL,   " Enter size and quality for a price" },
  { 14, 20, NORMAL, "SIZE      :" },
  { 16, 20, NORMAL, "QUALITY   :" },
  { 18, 18, NORMAL, "DIAMOND PRICE IS :" },
  { NULL, NULL, NULL, NULL },
};

static INPUT_FLD fields[] =
{ { 14, 30, 10, ERRLINE,ERRCOL },
  { 16, 30, 5, ERRLINE,ERRCOL },
};

put_screen(price_form);
diamond.size = get_float(&fields[0], 1.0, 0.0, 0.0);
diamond.quality = get_int(&fields[1], 4, 1, 1);

if ( (price = find_price(&diamond)) > 0.0 )
{ curset(18, 38);
  printf("%f", price);
}
else
    atsay(ERRLINE, ERRCOL, "Could not calculate price");

atsay(22, 20, "Press RETURN to continue");
gets(reply);
}
```

DEVELOPING LARGER SYSTEMS—A SUMMARY

We have completed the first major stage in the development of our client's system. Now, all further enhancements will be your responsibility. Some important points that you should have noticed in this chapter are:

1. More time was spent in thinking about and explaining the business case, the overall design, and the proper selection of tools than in actually coding.

2. A good tool is very general and highly reusable.

3. Very often a combination of top-down and bottom-up design can be used to create the same system.

4. By separating the task into several program files we have compartmentalized the overall tasks. The main functions of "gems.c" are very independent so that they can be coded by different people, then linked together for final testing. Furthermore, since the files are independent, we were able to test as we went.

5. By developing good tool sets initially, our work later on was simplified considerably.

6. The bigger and more complex the problem, the more likely that you will need to use structures to keep it under control.

APPENDIX A—
THE ASCII
CHARACTER CODE

000	NUL	032	SP	064	@	096	'
001	SOH	033	!	065	A	097	a
002	STH	034	"	066	B	098	b
003	ETX	035	#	067	C	099	c
004	EOT	036	$	068	D	100	d
005	ENQ	037	%	069	E	101	e
006	ACK	038	&	070	F	102	f
007	BEL	039	'	071	G	103	g
008	BS	040	(	072	H	104	h
009	HT	041	)	073	I	105	i
010	NL	042	*	074	J	106	j
011	VT	043	+	075	K	107	k
012	NP	044	,	076	L	108	l
013	CR	045	-	077	M	109	m
014	SO	046	.	078	N	110	n
015	SI	047	/	079	O	111	o
016	DLE	048	0	080	P	112	p
017	DC1	049	1	081	Q	113	q
018	DC2	050	2	082	R	114	r
019	DC3	051	3	083	S	115	s
020	DC4	052	4	084	T	116	t
021	NAK	053	5	085	U	117	u
022	SYN	054	6	086	V	118	v
023	ETB	055	7	087	W	119	w
024	CAN	056	8	088	X	120	x
025	EM	057	9	089	Y	121	y
026	SUB	058	:	090	Z	122	z
027	ESC	059	;	091	[	123	{
028	FS	060	<	092	\	124		
029	GS	061	=	093	]	125	}
030	RS	062	>	094	^	126	~
031	US	063	?	095	-	127	DEL

APPENDIX B—
PRECEDENCE AND ASSOCIATIVITY

Precedence	Operators	Associativity
high	() [] -> .	L to R
	++ -- * & - + ! sizeof (type) ~	R to L
	* / %	L to R
	+ -	L to R
	<< >>	L to R
	< > <= >=	L to R
	== !=	L to R
	&	L to R
	^	L to R
	|	L to R
	&&	L to R
	||	L to R
	?:	L to R
	= += &= >>= etc.	R to L
low	,	L to R

INDEX